The
WORST-CASE SCENARIO
2002 Survival Calendar

A WEEK-BY-WEEK GUIDE
TO SURVIVING A YEAR'S WORTH OF PERIL

By Joshua Piven and David Borgenicht

CHRONICLE BOOKS

ACKNOWLEDGMENTS: Many thanks to all of the experts who contributed their knowledge and experience to this calendar, as well as to Erin Slonaker, Mindy Brown, Jason Rekulak, and Jennifer Howie for their creative research and thinking, to Frances J. Soo Ping Chow for living and designing through it all, to Kerry Tessaro for her thoughtful editing, to Craig Hetzer for his creative vision, to Jay Schaefer for helping to start it all, and to the entire team at Chronicle Books.

ISBN 0-8118-3165-5

Printed in Hong Kong

Designed and produced by book soup publishing, inc.
Cover and interior design by Frances J. Soo Ping Chow
Typeset in Adobe Caslon and Helvetica
Illustrations by Brenda Brown
A book soup publishing book

Distributed in Canada by Raincoast Books
9050 Shaughnessy Street
Vancouver, B.C. V6P 6E5

Chronicle Books LLC
85 Second Street
San Francisco, CA 94105
www.chroniclebooks.com

Visit www.worstcasescenarios.com
for additional information, updates, and more.

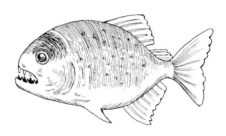

INTRODUCTION

"Life is either a daring adventure or nothing."
—Helen Keller

It's a whole new year—who knows what it holds in store?

Who knows what disaster or success tomorrow may bring? Who knows what's lurking behind the door, what's swimming beneath the surface, what might be around the corner?

But we can't spend today worrying about tomorrow. We can't sit in our houses waiting for the future to happen. Better to face it head on—with the courage, strength, and determination to take on (or fend off) whatever is thrown our way.

Four out of five survival experts agree that the keys to surviving any situation are the following:

• Be prepared.
• Do not panic.
• Have a plan.

The fifth expert, Bill Cosby, adds one more:

• "If you can find the humor in anything, you can survive it."

It is with those tips in mind that we have created this new edition of our calendar—a clear, step-by-step guide to staring danger in the face and coming out alive. Based on our best-selling books, *The Worst-Case Scenario Survival Handbook* and *The Worst-Case Scenario Survival Handbook: Travel*, this calendar contains dozens of new pieces of essential survival knowledge from the experts themselves—pilots, stuntmen, jungle survival experts, skydivers, safari operators, demolition derby drivers, and more. If the instructions amuse you as much as they educate, that's fine. (It's OK to laugh in the face of danger as long as you know what to do when the laughter subsides.)

Within these pages are steps you can follow to emerge relatively unscathed (or at the very least, alive) from dozens of life-threatening situations, with clear illustrations to help you through. From surviving a hit and run to escaping from killer bees, from controlling a runaway camel to jumping from roof to roof, from escaping a car teetering over the edge of a cliff to treating a scorpion sting, *The Worst-Case Scenario 2002 Survival Calendar* should, at the minimum, give you the confidence to follow the advice of the experts. To remain calm. To remain confident that you've got a plan. And to be ready for the best and worst the new year has to offer.

So read on, and plan your year accordingly. After all, life is the ultimate adventure. Live it well. Be prepared. And laugh in the face of danger.

Just hope that danger doesn't laugh back.

—The Authors

HOW TO JUMP FROM A BRIDGE OR CLIFF INTO A RIVER

1 Jump feet first.

2 Keep your body completely vertical.

3 Squeeze your feet together.

4 Enter the water feet first, and clench your buttocks together.
If you do not, water may rush in and cause severe internal damage.

5 Protect your crotch area by covering it with your hands.

6 Immediately after you hit the water, spread your arms and legs wide. Move them back and forth to generate resistance, which will slow your plunge to the bottom. Always assume the water is not deep enough to keep you from hitting bottom.

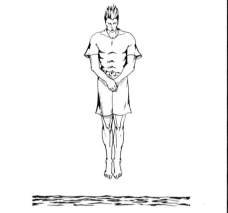

Jump feet first in a vertical position; squeeze your feet together; clench your backside and protect your crotch.

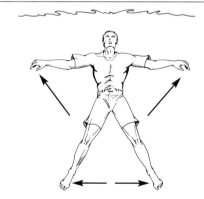

After you enter the water, spread your arms and legs wide and move them back and forth, which will help slow your descent.

DECEMBER/JANUARY

Monday	Tuesday	Wednesday
31	**1**	**2**
Annual Event: The Dakar Rally (the world's biggest off-road race) from Europe to Dakar, Senegal	**New Year's Day** 1735—Paul Revere is born.	

Thursday	Friday	Saturday *Last Quarter* ☽
3	**4**	**5**
		1933—Construction on the Golden Gate Bridge begins.

Sunday

6

1956—Mel Gibson is born.

1412—Joan of Arc is born.

★ Tip of the Week:

Hitting the water in this way could save your life, although it may break your legs. Moreover, if your body is not straight, you can break your back upon entry. Keep yourself vertical until you hit the water. Do not even think about going in headfirst unless you are absolutely sure that the water is at least 20 feet deep. If your legs hit the bottom, they will break. If your head hits, your skull will break.

December

S	M	T	W	T	F	S
						1
2	3	4	5	6	7	8
9	10	11	12	13	14	15
16	17	18	19	20	21	22
23/30	24/31	25	26	27	28	29

January

S	M	T	W	T	F	S
		1	2	3	4	5
6	7	8	9	10	11	12
13	14	15	16	17	18	19
20	21	22	23	24	25	26
27	28	29	30	31		

HOW TO DEAL
WITH ARMY ANTS

1 Dress appropriately when in army (or "worker") ant territory.
Wear long pants and tuck your pants into your boots or socks. You are likely to
encounter army ants in one of two ways: by inadvertently stepping into a march-
ing column or a foraging swarm; or when the raiding worker ants teem uninvited
through your camp.

2 Watch where you step.
Look beneath you for masses of ants and avoid stepping on them.

3 If the ants climb on you, step out of the column or mass of ants.

4 Jump up and down to dislodge the ants, and then pick the remaining ants
from your clothing and body.
If possible, sweep them off with a cloth or a stick.

5 If you are stung, treat the area as you would treat the sting of a bee or wasp.
Stings can produce intense burning and local pain, swelling, and itching. Apply
a cool compress to the sting area. Take an antibiotic if one is available. The use
of antihistamines and epinephrine may be required for individuals with an aller-
gy to ant venom.

JANUARY

Monday **7**	Tuesday **8**	Wednesday **9**
1904—CQD ("Come Quick Danger") radio distress signal is adopted. Predates SOS.		

Thursday **10**	Friday **11**	Saturday **12**
		1876—Jack London, author of *The Call of the Wild*, is born.

New Moon ●

Sunday 13

1946—First radio signal is transmitted to the moon.

★ **Tip of the Week:**

Army ants can be found in the tropical habitats of Central and South America and sub-Saharan Africa. Most species of army ants are subterranean, seldom seen, and for the most part, innocuous. Of the nearly 300 species that are distributed throughout the world's tropics and subtropics, no more than five species pose any problem for visitors.

January

S	M	T	W	T	F	S
		1	2	3	4	5
6	7	8	9	10	11	12
13	14	15	16	17	18	19
20	21	22	23	24	25	26
27	28	29	30	31		

HOW TO BUILD A SNOW CAVE

1 Find a large snow drift or snow bank on a slope.
Plan your cave with the opening at a right angle to the prevailing wind.

2 Dig a narrow tunnel into the slope (toward the back of the slope) and slightly upward.
Create a cavern big enough to lie in without touching the sides, roof, or ends.

3 Make the ceiling slightly dome-shaped.
A flat ceiling has no strength and in most cases will collapse before you are finished digging. The roof should be at least 12 inches thick. If you can see blue-green light (from filtered sunlight) through the top, the roof is too thin.

4 Put a small vent hole in the roof.
The hole will provide fresh air and a vent for a candle, if you are going to use one. Do not add any heat source larger than a small candle. Excessive heat will cause the ceiling to soften, drip, and weaken.

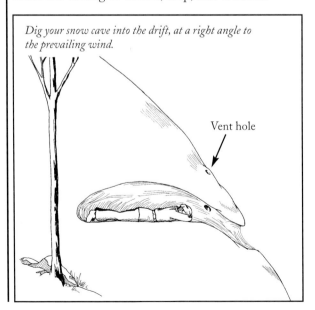

Dig your snow cave into the drift, at a right angle to the prevailing wind.

Vent hole

JANUARY

Monday **14**	Tuesday **15**	Wednesday **16**
	1929—Martin Luther King Jr. is born.	1773—Captain James Cook completes the first crossing of the Antarctic Circle.

Thursday **17**	Friday **18**	Saturday **19**
		1840—Antarctica is discovered by a Russian expedition.
		Sunday 20
1979—"I Will Survive" by Gloria Gaynor debuts this week on *Billboard*'s Top 40.	1896—The X-ray machine is exhibited for the first time, in New York City.	

★ **Tip of the Week:**

A preferable alternative to building a snow shelter is a man-made structure or vehicle. If none is available, search for anything that will help protect your body from heat loss. Caves, downed timber, or rock outcroppings can help protect you from the elements.

January

S	M	T	W	T	F	S
		1	2	3	4	5
6	7	8	9	10	11	12
13	14	15	16	17	18	19
20	21	22	23	24	25	26
27	28	29	30	31		

ESCAPING FROM BONDAGE

Upper Torso Bonds

- When your captors start binding you, take a deep breath, puff out your chest, and pull your shoulders back.
- Flex your arms against the bonds.
- When your captors are away, suck your chest and stomach in.
- Try to wiggle free with the extra room you have given yourself.

Leg and Ankle Bonds

- While being bound, flex your thighs, knees, calves, and ankles against the bonds.
- If being bound at ankles, force them apart by bracing your toes and knees together. Use the same technique if your wrists are being bound.
- If being bound at thighs and calves, force them apart by keeping your toes together and your legs turned slightly outward.
- Free yourself by relaxing your legs and working the bonds down.
- Try to use your hands, even if they are bound.

Take a deep breath.

Flex against your bonds.

Keep your wrists apart.

Brace toes and knees together.

JANUARY

Monday *First Quarter* ☾ **21**	Tuesday **22**	Wednesday **23**
Martin Luther King Jr. Day		1950—Richard Dean Anderson, from TV's *MacGyver*, is born.
Thursday **24**	Friday **25**	Saturday **26**
		Sunday **27**
	1890—Traveling by boat, train, and horse, Nellie Bly completes the first solo around-the-world journey by a woman, in 72 days, 6 hours, and 11 minutes.	

★ **Tip of the Week:**

Even a small amount of slack can allow you enough room to work free of your bonds. Usually, you can get even more room by bracing against the rope. A long rope that is wrapped around you offers more hope of escape than short bonds tied at key points. Try to work the rope loose where bonds overlap.

January

S	M	T	W	T	F	S
			1	2	3	4	5
6	7	8	9	10	11	12
13	14	15	16	17	18	19
20	21	22	23	24	25	26
27	28	29	30	31		

HOW TO BUILD AN ANIMAL TRAP

Use a holding trap (or snare) to trap small ground animals. Holding traps capture animals but do not kill them—you will need to do this yourself.

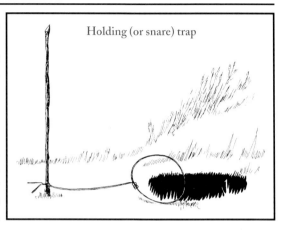

Holding (or snare) trap

1 Procure a two-foot-long wire and make a loop at one end. Wire is essential—animals can bite through string and twine. Use a small stick to aid in making the loop, by wrapping the wire around the stick and then removing the stick.

2 Take the other end of the wire and pass it through the loop.
This will make a snare loop, which becomes a snare that will tighten as the animal struggles. The snare loop should be about five inches in diameter.

3 Twist and tie the end of the wire to a one-foot stake.

4 Place the snare in an animal track or at the entrance to an animal burrow or hole.
You can also use two snares, one behind the other, to increase your odds of catching something. The struggling animal caught in one snare will likely become caught in the other.

5 Anchor the stake in the ground.
Position the stake in an area where the animal won't see it. Mark it so that you can find it later.

JANUARY/FEBRUARY

Monday *Full Moon* ○	Tuesday	Wednesday
28	**29**	**30**
1915—U.S. Coast Guard is created. Their motto: *Semper Paratus* (Always Ready).		1835—Andrew Jackson survives the first presidential assassination attempt.

Thursday	Friday	Saturday
31	**1**	**2**
		Groundhog Day
		Sunday
		3
1851—Evaporated milk, now used frequently in expeditions, is invented.	National Canned Food Month begins.	

★ **Tip of the Week:**

Check the trap only once or twice daily; checking it too often may frighten away the animals.

January

S	M	T	W	T	F	S
		1	2	3	4	5
6	7	8	9	10	11	12
13	14	15	16	17	18	19
20	21	22	23	24	25	26
27	28	29	30	31		

February

S	M	T	W	T	F	S
					1	2
3	4	5	6	7	8	9
10	11	12	13	14	15	16
17	18	19	20	21	22	23
24	25	26	27	28		

HOW TO SURVIVE IN FRIGID WATER

1 Do not attempt to swim unless it is for a very short distance.
A strong swimmer has a 50-50 chance of surviving a 50-yard swim in 50-degree Fahrenheit water. Swim only if you can reach land, a boat, or a floating object with a few strokes. Swimming moves cold water over skin, causing rapid cooling.

2 If you are wearing a flotation device, assume the heat escape lessening posture (HELP).
Cross your ankles, draw your knees to your chest, and cross your arms over your chest. Your hands should be kept high on your chest or neck to keep them warm. Do not remove clothing. Clothes will not weigh you down but will hold warm water against your skin like a diver's wetsuit. This position can reduce heat loss by 50 percent.

3 If two or more people are in the water and all are wearing flotation devices, assume the "huddle" position.
Two to four people should "hug," with chest touching chest. This position allows body heat to be shared. Also, rescuers can spot groups more easily than individuals.

If two or more people are in the water together, assume the huddle position, hugging chest to chest.

4 Keep movement to a minimum.
Increasing the heart rate speeds body cooling. Try to breathe normally.

5 Once you are rescued, watch for signs of hypothermia.
Slurred speech and a lack of shivering are signs of severe body temperature loss. Immediately rewarm your body in a warm water bath (100–105°F), keeping extremities out of the water, or use the body heat of another person to rewarm. Do not rub extremities in an attempt to warm them; tissue damage could occur.

FEBRUARY

Monday *Last Quarter* ☽
4

1932—First winter Olympic Games open in Lake Placid, New York.

Tuesday
5

Wednesday
6

1933—Highest recorded sea wave (not a tsunami) occurs during a Pacific hurricane near Manila; it measures 34 meters.

Thursday
7

Friday
8

Saturday
9

Sunday
10

1828—Jules Verne is born.

1910—Boy Scouts of America is founded. Their motto: Be prepared.

Boy Scouts Day (observed)
1863—The fire extinguisher is patented.

★ **Tip of the Week:**

If you are not wearing a flotation device, find something—a piece of driftwood or floating cooler—to use as a flotation device. Float on your back or try to assume the HELP position.

February

S	M	T	W	T	F	S
					1	2
3	4	5	6	7	8	9
10	11	12	13	14	15	16
17	18	19	20	21	22	23
24	25	26	27	28		

ERNEST SHACKLETON

In August 1914, British explorer Sir Ernest Shackleton and his crew set sail for Antarctica—unwittingly beginning the most incredible survival story of the twentieth century. Five months later, their ship, the *Endurance*, was trapped in shifting arctic ice. With no radio and no civilization within a thousand miles, the crew could only wait and hope that their boat would be released.

Nine months later, they watched in horror as shifting ice packs shattered their ship, which sank into the ocean. Never one to give up, Shackleton ordered his men to march toward South George Island, a whaling base more than 800 miles away. They spent the next five months dragging lifeboats and supplies over the frigid landscape, averaging 1.5 miles a day. To keep up morale, the men sang songs and held dogsled races.

In April 1916, they reached open water, and Shackleton and five others set sail in an open boat with only a sextant to guide them. After 17 days on stormy seas, they landed on the island, only to discover they still had to trek over miles of uncharted glaciers—with no rations and no equipment save a 50-foot rope. Despite overwhelming odds, they reached their destination, and the rest of their crew was rescued a few weeks later.

Imagine hundreds of nights in wet sleeping bags in sub-zero temperatures—without Gore-Tex, without Powerbars, and without a single casualty among all 28 men. This week, we honor the birth of Sir Ernest Shackleton—fearless explorer, leader among men, and true survivor.

FEBRUARY

Monday *New Moon* ●
11

1752—Pennsylvania Hospital, the first hospital in the U.S., officially opens in Philadelphia.

Tuesday
12

1809—Abraham Lincoln is born.

Wednesday
13

Ash Wednesday

Thursday
14

Valentine's Day

Friday
15

1874—Ernest Shackleton, captain of the *Endurance*, is born.

Saturday
16

Sunday
17

★ **Tip of the Week:**
To avoid frostbite and frostnip, keep extremities warm and covered during cold weather. Use layered clothing and a face mask. Wear mittens instead of gloves, and keep the ears covered. Take breaks from the cold in order to warm extremities whenever possible.

February

S	M	T	W	T	F	S
					1	2
3	4	5	6	7	8	9
10	11	12	13	14	15	16
17	18	19	20	21	22	23
24	25	26	27	28		

HOW TO FOOL
A LIE DETECTOR TEST

1 During the pre-test, force yourself to breath faster than normal.
Examiners will administer a pre-test before the actual polygraph to create a baseline of reactions. Breathing faster will skew the results to make you appear "normal" when nervous.

2 During the pre-test, display confidence. Never appear nervous or shy.

3 Maintain eye contact with the examiner. Do not fidget or otherwise appear nervous.
Do not, however, sit completely still. Move something subtly but regularly: your toes, fingers, hips, etc.

4 Do not try to anticipate the questions you will be asked. Think positive and relaxing thoughts.

5 When answering control questions truthfully, bite your tongue slightly.
This will hopefully give a false reading—they may find that it is impossible to decipher your test because the readings are inconsistent (answers show stress both when you're answering truthfully and when you could be lying).

FEBRUARY

Monday **18**	Tuesday **19**	Wednesday **20** _First Quarter_ ☾
Presidents' Day 1978—The first Ironman Triathlon World Championship (swim 2.4 miles, bike 112 miles, run 26.2 miles) is held in Hawaii.		1872—Hydraulic electric elevator is patented by Cyrus Baldwin.

Thursday **21**	Friday **22**	Saturday **23**
		Sunday **24**
	1732—George Washington is born.	1868—First impeachment proceeding against a U.S. President (Andrew Johnson) begins.

★ **Tip of the Week:**

Remember that a lie detector test is subject to interpretation, and a test is only as good as the examiner. If the examiner deems the results inconclusive, you will likely not be required to pass another lie detector test.

February

S	M	T	W	T	F	S
					1	2
3	4	5	6	7	8	9
10	11	12	13	14	15	16
17	18	19	20	21	22	23
24	25	26	27	28		

HOW TO SURVIVE IN WHITEWATER RAPIDS WHEN YOU FALL OUT OF YOUR RAFT

1 If you are thrown from the raft, lie on your back, face up, with your feet facing downstream.
This will protect your head in the event you hit rocks, and your life jacket should help to keep you afloat.

2 If your raft is still accessible, swim for it, and hold on.
Even if it is upside down, it can still provide protection from rocks and other obstacles.

3 Be aware of the current and of river conditions.
If you get to a "flat water" section of the river (a calm area between rapids), vigorously swim for the shore.

4 Be prepared for a "hole" in the river.
This is a dangerous area where water recirculates, creating a whirlpool that can hold you under. Generally, in a hole, the surface water flows upstream, but deeper water continues to move downstream.

5 If you encounter a hole, do not continue to float—plunge your feet down as far as you can and actively swim to the bottom.
Upon reaching the deeper, downstream-flowing water, you will be pulled from the hole by the current.

FEBRUARY/MARCH

Monday
25

Tuesday
26

Wednesday
27

Full Moon ○

1919—Congress establishes Grand Canyon National Park.

Thursday
28

Friday
1

Saturday
2

Sunday
3

American Red Cross Month begins.

1872—Yellowstone, the nation's first national park, is established.

1513—Ponce de León begins his quest for the Fountain of Youth.

★ **Tip of the Week:**

Whenever you are rafting or kayaking in whitewater, always wear your life jacket and a helmet.

February						
S	M	T	W	T	F	S
					1	2
3	4	5	6	7	8	9
10	11	12	13	14	15	16
17	18	19	20	21	22	23
24	25	26	27	28		

March						
S	M	T	W	T	F	S
					1	2
3	4	5	6	7	8	9
10	11	12	13	14	15	16
17	18	19	20	21	22	23
24/31	25	26	27	28	29	30

HOW TO ESCAPE FROM A CAR HANGING OVER THE EDGE OF A CLIFF

1 Do not shift your weight or make any sudden movements.

2 If the front doors are still over land, use these doors to make your escape, regardless of which way your car is facing.
Open the door gradually and slowly get out of the car.

3 If the front doors are over the edge, move to the rear of the car. Proceed slowly and deliberately; do not jump or lurch. If you have a steering wheel lock or a screwdriver, take it with you.

4 If you think that opening the rear doors will cause the car to slide over the edge, you must break the window.
Without shifting your weight or rocking the car, use the steering wheel lock or screwdriver to shatter the rear window. Hit it in the center—the window is made of safety glass and will not injure you.

5 Get out as quickly as possible.

If the front doors are over the edge of the cliff, move slowly to the rear of the car and exit through a rear door.

MARCH

Monday	Tuesday *Last Quarter* ☽	Wednesday
4	**5**	**6**
1902—American Automobile Association (AAA) is founded.	1872—George Westinghouse patents the air brake—crucial to trains, trucks, and buses.	1836—Siege at the Alamo ends. No one survives.

Thursday	Friday	Saturday
7	**8**	**9**
		1454—Amerigo Vespucci is born.

Sunday

10

★ **Tip of the Week:**

If the driver and passengers are in both front and rear seats, the people who are closest to the edge of the cliff should attempt to get out of the car first, moving simultaneously.

March

S	M	T	W	T	F	S
					1	2
3	4	5	6	7	8	9
10	11	12	13	14	15	16
17	18	19	20	21	22	23
24/31	25	26	27	28	29	30

HOW TO TAKE A PUNCH

In the Stomach

1 Tighten your stomach muscles. A body blow to the gut (solar plexus) can damage organs and kill. This sort of punch is one of the best and easiest ways to knock someone out. (Harry Houdini died from an unexpected blow to the abdomen.)

2 Do not suck in your stomach if you expect that a punch is imminent.
Sucking in increases the risk of internal injury.

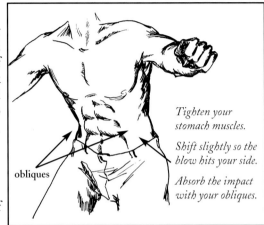

Tighten your stomach muscles.

Shift slightly so the blow hits your side.

Absorb the impact with your obliques.

obliques

3 If you cannot avoid the punch altogether, shift slightly so that the blow hits your side, but do not flinch or move away from the punch.
Moving away only gives the punch more momentum. Try to absorb the blow with your obliques, the set of muscles on your side that wraps around your ribs. While a blow to this area may crack a rib, it is less likely to do damage to internal organs.

In the Head

1 Move toward the blow, not away from it.
Getting punched while moving backward will result in the head taking the punch at full force. A punch to the face can cause head whipping, where the brain moves suddenly inside the skull, and can cause severe injury or death.

2 Tighten your neck muscles and clench your jaw to avoid scraping of the upper and lower palates.

MARCH

Monday 11	Tuesday 12	Wednesday 13 *New Moon* ●
		1999—Boxers Evander Holyfield and Lennox Lewis fight for the Undisputed Heavyweight Championship; it ends in a controversial draw.
	1912—Girl Scouts of America is founded.	

Thursday 14	Friday 15	Saturday 16
		Sunday 17
	1937—The nation's first blood bank is established in Chicago.	St. Patrick's Day

★ **Tip of the Week:**

You can absorb a punch to the head most effectively and with the least injury by taking it in the forehead. Avoid taking the punch in the nose, which is extremely painful.

March

S	M	T	W	T	F	S
					1	2
3	4	5	6	7	8	9
10	11	12	13	14	15	16
17	18	19	20	21	22	23
24/31	25	26	27	28	29	30

HOW TO JUMP FROM A BUILDING INTO A DUMPSTER

1 Jump straight down.
If you leap off and away from the building at an angle, your trajectory will make you miss the Dumpster. Resist your natural tendency to push off.

2 Tuck your head and bring your legs around.
To do this during the fall, execute a three-quarter revolution—basically, a not-quite-full somersault. This is the only method that will allow a proper landing, with your back facing down.

3 Aim for the center of the Dumpster.

4 Land flat on your back so that when your body folds, your feet and hands meet.
When your body hits any surface from a significant height, the body folds into a V. This means landing on your stomach can result in a broken back.

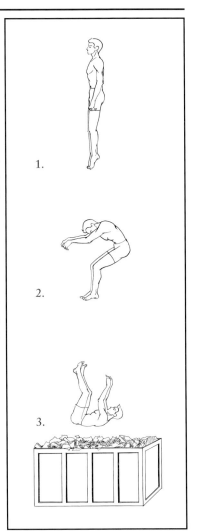

1.

2.

3.

MARCH

Monday **18**	Tuesday **19**	Wednesday **20**
	1955—Bruce Willis is born.	Vernal Equinox

Thursday *First Quarter* ☾ **21**	Friday **22**	Saturday **23**
		Sunday **24**
1871—Stanley begins his expedition in Africa to find Dr. Livingstone.		Palm Sunday

★ **Tip of the Week:**

It is entirely possible to survive a high fall (five stories or more) into a Dumpster, provided the Dumpster is filled with the right type of trash (cardboard boxes are best) and you land correctly. Be aware of what may be in the Dumpster—it could be filled with bricks or other unfriendly materials.

March

S	M	T	W	T	F	S
					1	2
3	4	5	6	7	8	9
10	11	12	13	14	15	16
17	18	19	20	21	22	23
24/31	25	26	27	28	29	30

HOW TO AVOID AND SURVIVE A HIT AND RUN

1   Always cross streets in a crosswalk and look both ways before crossing.

2   Keep your eyes on both the traffic patterns and the oncoming cars.
Be familiar with the intersection, and know which cars have a green light and which do not. Use the lights to help you cross, but pay more attention to the moving cars—they may not be paying attention to you, or the lights.

3   If a car is headed directly for you, assess the amount of time you have.

4   Dive and roll out of the car's path if you have enough time before impact. You may get some cuts and bruises but you will not get run over.

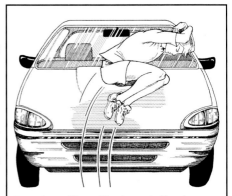

5   If you can't get out of the way, jump as high as you can just before impact. Jump in a tight tuck or ball position, with your arms over your head. Jump in profile with your shoulder toward the car; this exposes fewer vital organs.

Jump in profile, tucking into a ball and covering your head. Roll onto and off the windshield.

6   Brace for impact.
You will probably hit the windshield.

7   Roll onto and off the windshield.

8   Stay rolled into a ball and brace yourself for when you hit the ground. Keep your arms over your head.

9   Try to roll or crawl out of the way of any other cars that might be approaching from both directions.

MARCH

Monday	Tuesday	Wednesday
25	**26**	**27**
	1845—Patent for adhesive medicated plaster for treatment of broken bones is issued.	

Thursday *Full Moon* ○	Friday	Saturday
28	**29**	**30**
		1831—Anesthesia is first used in surgery.
		Sunday
		31
		Easter
Passover	Good Friday	1932—The Ford Motor Company unveils its V-8 engine.

★ **Tip of the Week:**

If the vehicle is a large truck (an 18-wheeler) with high clearance and you cannot get out of the way, lie flat, face-down on the ground, feet first, in the same direction as the truck. Try to center yourself between the wheels, and the truck may pass safely over you. Protect your head in case the truck is dragging something beneath it.

March

S	M	T	W	T	F	S
					1	2
3	4	5	6	7	8	9
10	11	12	13	14	15	16
17	18	19	20	21	22	23
24/31	25	26	27	28	29	30

HOW TO BREAK DOWN A DOOR

INTERIOR DOORS

 Give the door a well-placed kick or two to the lock area to break it down. Running at the door and slamming against it with your shoulder or body is not usually as effective as kicking with your foot. Your foot exerts more force than your shoulder, and you will be able to direct this force toward the area of the locking mechanism more effectively this way.

EXTERIOR DOORS

 Give the door several well-placed kicks at the point where the lock is mounted.
An exterior door usually takes several tries to break down this way, so keep at it.

Alternative Method (if you have a sturdy piece of steel):
Wrench or pry the lock off the door by inserting the tool between the lock and the door and prying back and forth.

Exterior doors are of sturdier construction. Kick at the point where the lock is mounted.

APRIL

Monday **1**	Tuesday **2**	Wednesday **3**
April Fools' Day		

Thursday **4** *Last Quarter* ☽	Friday **5**	Saturday **6**
		1909—Admiral Robert Peary becomes the first man to reach the North Pole.

		Sunday **7**
1821—Linus Yale (inventor of locks) is born.	1971—Fran Phipps becomes the first woman to reach the North Pole.	1954—Jackie Chan is born.

★ Tip of the Week:

You can usually determine the construction and solidity of a door by tapping on it. If it sounds hollow or tinny, it will require a moderate amount of force to break down. If it sounds solid, it will require a significantly greater amount of force, or some sort of pry bar.

April

S	M	T	W	T	F	S
	1	2	3	4	5	6
7	8	9	10	11	12	13
14	15	16	17	18	19	20
21	22	23	24	25	26	27
28	29	30				

HOW TO SURVIVE
A MUGGING

1 Do not argue or fight with a mugger unless your life is clearly in danger.
If all a mugger wants is your purse, wallet, or other belongings, surrender them.
Your possessions are not worth your life.

2 If you are certain that your attacker means to do you or a loved one harm,
attack vital areas of your assailant's body.
Aim to disable your attacker with the first blow by:
- Thrusting your fingers into and above your attacker's eyes.
- Driving your knee in an upward direction into his groin (if the mugger
  is male).
- Striking the front of your attacker's throat, using the area between your
  thumb and first finger, or the side of your hand, held straight and strong.
- Slamming your elbow into the mugger's ribs.
- Stomping down on the mugger's instep.

3 Use an object as a weapon.
Many common objects can be effective weapons if they are aimed at vulnerable
body parts. Pick up and use what is easily available, whether it is a stick, your
keys, or a car antenna (all are good for slashing or jabbing at your attacker's face
and eyes).

APRIL

Monday 8	Tuesday 9	Wednesday 10
	1872—Dried milk is patented.	1849—The safety pin is patented.

Thursday 11	Friday *New Moon* ● 12	Saturday 13

Sunday
14

1865—Lincoln is shot at Ford's Theatre.

1912—The *Titanic* sinks—711 people survive.

1970—*Apollo 13* takes off.

★ **Tip of the Week:**

To foil a pickpocket, carry a wallet that contains only a small amount of money and photo ID that is not your driver's license or passport. Use this wallet for daily small expenses. Wrap a rubber band around it so you will feel it if someone attempts to remove it.

April

S	M	T	W	T	F	S
	1	2	3	4	5	6
7	8	9	10	11	12	13
14	15	16	17	18	19	20
21	22	23	24	25	26	27
28	29	30				

THE *APOLLO 13* SPACE MISSION

"Houston, we've had a problem here."

Two days after the liftoff of *Apollo 13*, James Lovell, John Swigert, and Fred Haise were enjoying a smooth ride, but they had not yet landed on the moon. Suddenly, disaster struck: An oxygen tank exploded, seriously damaging the service module. Clouds of oxygen vented into space, leaving the crew with only the smaller lunar module's oxygen stores. The situation was dire: The spacecraft's supply of electricity, light, and water was lost, and the astronauts were 200,000 miles from Earth—with no sure method for getting home.

To survive the mission, they quickly retreated to the lunar module and shut down all non-critical systems in the command module. But the lunar module was designed to support only two men for two days, not three men for four days. Could they last until they fired up the command module for reentry into the Earth's atmosphere?

Within a day, carbon dioxide levels were rising dangerously, as the filters in the lunar module were different from those in the command module. So they improvised—with Mission Control's direction, the crew fashioned their own filters using plastic bags, duct tape, and socks.

To make the most of their limited consumable supplies, the crew cut back severely on water and food, losing a combined 31 pounds.

Meanwhile, on the ground in Houston, Texas, Mission Control rushed to devise a plan for reentry. They successfully directed Lovell to use the sun to align the spacecraft, and the module and its crew returned safely to Earth on April 17, 1970.

This week, we celebrate the astronauts of *Apollo 13*. They are true survivors.

APRIL

Monday **15**	Tuesday **16**	Wednesday **17**
	1786—Sir John Franklin, discoverer of the Northwest Passage, is born.	1970—*Apollo 13* crew lands safely.

Thursday **18**	Friday **19**	Saturday *First Quarter* ☾ **20**
		1770—Captain James Cook discovers New South Wales.
		Sunday **21**
1906—The San Francisco earthquake hits.		

★ **Tip of the Week:**

Creative, calm thinking is the key to surviving a crisis. Don't panic, remember all the lessons you've learned, and trust that you will be successful.

April

S	M	T	W	T	F	S
	1	2	3	4	5	6
7	8	9	10	11	12	13
14	15	16	17	18	19	20
21	22	23	24	25	26	27
28	29	30				

HOW TO SURVIVE IF YOUR PARACHUTE FAILS TO OPEN

1 Signal to a jumping companion that you're having a malfunction. Wave your arms and point to your chute.

2 When your companion (and new best friend) gets to you, hook arms.

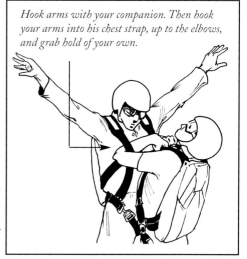

Hook arms with your companion. Then hook your arms into his chest strap, up to the elbows, and grab hold of your own.

3 Once you are hooked together, the two of you will still be falling at terminal velocity, about 130 mph. When your friend opens his chute, there will be no way either of you will be able to hold onto one another normally, because the G-forces will triple or quadruple your body weight. To combat this, hook your arms into his chest strap, or through the two sides of the front of his harness, all the way up to your elbows. Then grab hold of your own harness.

4 Open the chute.

5 The chute opening shock will be severe, probably enough to dislocate or break your arms.
Your friend now must hold on to you with one arm while steering his canopy (the part of the chute that controls direction and speed).

6 If your friend's canopy is slow and big, you may hit the grass or dirt slowly enough to break only a leg, and your chances of survival are high.

7 If there is a body of water nearby, head for that.
Once you hit the water, you will have to tread with just your legs, and hope that your partner is able to pull you out.

APRIL

Monday **22**	Tuesday **23**	Wednesday **24**
		1880—Vega Day (Sweden): The first person to sail the Eurasian continent returns home.

Thursday **25**	Friday **26** *Full Moon* ○	Saturday **27**
		1791—Samuel Morse is born.
		Sunday **28**
		1919—First intentional jump from an airplane using a parachute is made.

★ **Tip of the Week:**

Check your chute before you jump. The good news is that today's parachutes are built to open, so even if you make big mistakes packing them, they tend to sort themselves out. Make sure that the parachute is folded in straight lines—that there are no twists—and that the slider is positioned correctly to keep the parachute from opening too fast.

April

S	M	T	W	T	F	S
		1	2	3	4	5	6
7	8	9	10	11	12	13
14	15	16	17	18	19	20
21	22	23	24	25	26	27
28	29	30				

HOW TO JUMP
FROM A MOVING TRAIN

1 Make your jump from the end of the last (the rear) car.

If this is not an option, you can jump from the space between cars, or from the door if you can get it open.

2 Wait for the train to slow as it rounds a bend in the tracks, if you have time.

3 Pick your landing spot before you jump.

The ideal spot is relatively soft and free of obstructions. Avoid trees, bushes, and rocks.

4 Get as low to the floor as possible, bending your knees so you can leap away from the train car.

5 Jump perpendicular to the train, leaping as far away from the train as you can.

6 Cover and protect your head with your hands and arms, and roll like a log when you land.

Do NOT roll head over heels as if doing a forward somersault.

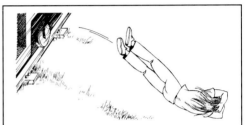

Pick your landing spot, and jump as far away from the train as you can. Protect your head.

Try to land so that all parts of your body hit the ground at the same time.

Roll like a log, keeping your head protected.

APRIL/MAY

Monday
29

Tuesday
30

1900—Casey Jones, the ill-fated train engineer, leaves Memphis for Canton.

Wednesday
1

May Day

Thursday
2

1919—First domestic American flight service begins.

Friday
3

Saturday
4

Last Quarter ☽

Sunday
5

1865—First U.S. train robbery occurs.

★ **Tip of the Week:**

To soften the blow, stuff blankets, clothing, or seat cushions underneath your clothes if they are available. Wear a thick jacket if possible. Use a belt to secure some padding around your head, but make certain you can see clearly. Pad your knees, elbows, and hips.

			April			
S	M	T	W	T	F	S
	1	2	3	4	5	6
7	8	9	10	11	12	13
14	15	16	17	18	19	20
21	22	23	24	25	26	27
28	29	30				

			May			
S	M	T	W	T	F	S
				1	2	3	4
5	6	7	8	9	10	11
12	13	14	15	16	17	18
19	20	21	22	23	24	25
26	27	28	29	30	31	

HOW TO SURVIVE IF YOU ARE ATTACKED BY LEECHES

1 Do not attempt to remove a leech by pulling up on its middle section or by using salt, heat, or insect repellent.
Dislodging by squeezing, salting, burning, or otherwise annoying the leech while it is feeding will cause it to regurgitate, most likely spreading the bacteria from its digestive system into your open wound, causing infection.

2 Identify the anterior (oral) sucker.
Look for the small end of the leech. A common mistake is to go immediately to the large sucker.

3 Place a fingernail on your skin (not on the leech itself), directly adjacent to the oral sucker.

4 Gently but firmly slide your finger toward where the leech is feeding and push the sucker away sideways.
When the seal made by the oral sucker is broken, the leech will stop feeding. After the oral sucker has been dislodged, the leech's head will seek to reattach, and it may attach to the finger that displaced the head. Even if the oral sucker attaches again, the leech does not begin to feed immediately.

5 Displace the posterior (hind) sucker.
While continuing to flick occasionally at the head end, push at or pick under the hind sucker with a fingernail to cause it to lose its suction.

6 Dispose of the leech.
Once the leech is detached, you can put salt or insect repellent directly on it to keep it from attaching to anything else.

7 Treat the wound.
Keep the area clean, and cover it with a small bandage if necessary. If itching becomes severe, take an antihistamine.

MAY

Monday	Tuesday	Wednesday
6	**7**	**8**
1937—The *Hindenburg* zeppelin explodes.	1992—The longest deep-water dive is completed by Richard Presley.	1541—Hernando De Soto reaches the Mississippi River and is the first European to cross it.

Thursday	Friday	Saturday
9	**10**	**11**

		Sunday *New Moon* ●
		12
	1497—Amerigo Vespucci sets sail for the New World.	**Mother's Day** 1820—Florence Nightingale is born.

★ **Tip of the Week:**

Leeches need a solid surface to hold onto even when they are not feeding. Avoid leeches by staying in the open: Swim in deep, open water, avoid boat docks, and do not wade through areas with submerged branches or rocks. In jungles, remain on trails and be aware of leeches on overhanging branches and vines.

May

S	M	T	W	T	F	S
			1	2	3	4
5	6	7	8	9	10	11
12	13	14	15	16	17	18
19	20	21	22	23	24	25
26	27	28	29	30	31	

HOW TO FIND YOUR DIRECTION WITHOUT A COMPASS

What You Need:
An analog watch
A six-inch stick

NORTHERN HEMISPHERE

1 Place a small stick vertically in the ground so that it casts a shadow.

2 Place your watch on the ground so that the hour hand points along the shadow of the stick.

3 Find the point on the watch midway between the hour hand and 12:00. If the watch is on Daylight Savings Time—which is during most of the summer—use the midway point between the hour hand and 1:00.

4 Draw an imaginary line from that point through the center of the watch. This imaginary line is a north-south line. The sun will be more to one side than the other; this is south.

SOUTHERN HEMISPHERE

★ Place your watch on the ground so that 12:00 points along the shadow. Find the midway point between the hour hand and 12:00. Draw an imaginary line from the point through the center of the watch. This is the north-south line, with the sun toward the north.

MAY

Monday **13**	Tuesday **14**	Wednesday **15**
1607—Jamestown, the first colony, is founded in Virginia.	1804—Lewis and Clark expedition begins.	
Thursday **16**	Friday **17**	Saturday **18**
		1953—Jacqueline Cochran becomes first woman to break the sound barrier.
		Sunday *First Quarter* ☽ **19**

★ **Tips of the Week:**
- You can also get a sense for direction by paying attention to the movement of clouds: Generally, weather moves from east to west.
- Moss tends to grow on the north side of trees and rocks, so be aware of any trends in moss growth where you are.

May

S	M	T	W	T	F	S
				1	2	3	4
5	6	7	8	9	10	11
12	13	14	15	16	17	18
19	20	21	22	23	24	25
26	27	28	29	30	31	

HOW TO ESCAPE FROM AN ALLIGATOR

1 Do not swim or wade alone in alligator-infested waters.

2 Never feed alligators.
In most attack cases, humans had fed the alligators prior to the attack. This is an important link: Feeding alligators seems to cause them to lose their fear of humans and make them more aggressive.

3 Do not dangle arms and legs from boats, and avoid throwing unused bait or fish from a boat or dock.

4 Do not harass, try to touch, or capture any alligator. Leave babies and eggs alone. Any adult alligator will respond to a distress call from any youngster. Mother alligators guarding nests and babies will defend them.

To get an alligator to release something it has in its mouth, tap it on the snout.

5 If you are attacked, go for the eyes and nose.
Use any weapon you have, or your fist.

6 If its jaws are closed on something you want to remove (for example, a limb), tap or punch it on the snout.
Alligators often open their mouths when tapped lightly. They may drop whatever it is they have taken hold of and back off.

MAY

Monday
20

Victoria Day (Canada)

1893—St. Augustine Alligator Farm opens in Florida.

Tuesday
21

1881—American Red Cross is organized by Clara Barton.

1927—Charles Lindbergh is first to complete a nonstop transatlantic flight.

Wednesday
22

Thursday
23

1879—Iowa State University establishes the first veterinary school in the U.S.

Friday
24

Saturday
25

1721—The first insurance policy becomes available in the U.S.

Sunday   *Full Moon* ○
26

1907—John Wayne is born.

★ **Tip of the Week:**

If the alligator gets you in its jaws and you cannot force its mouth open by using this technique, try to keep the alligator's mouth clamped shut so that it does not begin shaking or rolling (which can cause severe tissue damage).

May

S	M	T	W	T	F	S
			1	2	3	4
5	6	7	8	9	10	11
12	13	14	15	16	17	18
19	20	21	22	23	24	25
26	27	28	29	30	31	

HOW TO SURVIVE
A FLASH FLOOD

1 If inside, check the water level outside.
If it is deeper than one foot, do not attempt to drive away. Cars can be swept away in as little as two feet of water.

2 If the water inside is not rising quickly or flowing fast, turn off the power to the building and stay indoors.
Only enter a basement if the water is not rising fast. Turn off gas at the main valve to the building. If the water is knee deep, never enter the basement—you may become trapped and drown.

3 If the water level outside is deeper than three feet or seems to be rising or flowing quickly, evacuate the building.

4 Find a flotation device for each person leaving the building.
These can be personal flotation devices (lifejackets) or, if unavailable, couch or chair cushions. Plastic, sealable bags filled with air and placed under a tucked shirt can also provide flotation.

5 Leave the building and move to higher ground.
Do not attempt to drive a car in standing water more than half a foot deep. Proceed to higher ground on foot or in a boat, depending on the depth of water.

Monday **27**	Tuesday **28**	Wednesday **29**
		1953—Sir Edmund Hillary and Sherpa Tenzing Norgay become the first explorers to reach the summit of Mount Everest.
Memorial Day Observed		

Thursday **30**	Friday **31**	Saturday **1**
		National Safety Month begins. 1831—The magnetic North Pole is located by James Clark Ross.
		Sunday *Last Quarter* ☽ **2**
Memorial Day	1889—The Johnstown Flood, the worst in U.S. history, takes place in southwest Pennsylvania.	

★ **Tip of the Week:**

After the flood, wear boots and waders when reentering buildings. Do not eat any food that was in the flood, including canned goods; flood waters carry chemicals and disease. Pump out flooded basements gradually (about one-third of the water per day) to avoid structural damage.

		May								June				
S	**M**	**T**	**W**	**T**	**F**	**S**		**S**	**M**	**T**	**W**	**T**	**F**	**S**
				1	2	3	4							1
5	6	7	8	9	10	11		2	3	4	5	6	7	8
12	13	14	15	16	17	18		9	10	11	12	13	14	15
19	20	21	22	23	24	25		16	17	18	19	20	21	22
26	27	28	29	30	31			23/30	24	25	26	27	28	29

HOW TO SURVIVE WHEN YOU FALL INTO A CESSPOOL

1 Get out quickly.
In cases of falls into cesspools and septic tanks, the most common cause of death is asphyxiation from methane gas. An empty tank can be as dangerous as a full one. The methane gas that is common in septic systems causes rapid unconsciousness; deaths in as little as two minutes have been recorded.

2 Hold your breath for as long as possible between breaths.

3 If you cannot climb out, give one loud shout for help.
Tanks and cesspools currently in use will be full nearly to the top with liquid and solid waste. Do not shout repeatedly—this will deplete your air supply.

4 Once out, get at least 10 feet away from the tank before trying to catch your breath.

JUNE

Monday **3**	Tuesday **4**	Wednesday **5**
	1892—The Sierra Club is incorporated. 1963—Jimmy Hoffa is indicted.	

Thursday **6**	Friday **7**	Saturday **8**
		Sunday **9**
1938—Superman first appears in DC Comics.	1769—Daniel Boone begins exploring Kentucky.	

★ **Tip of the Week:**

If another person has fallen into a cesspool or tank, do not jump in to try to rescue them. Hold your breath and hold out a pole or rope to the victim while someone calls 911.

June

S	M	T	W	T	F	S
						1
2	3	4	5	6	7	8
9	10	11	12	13	14	15
16	17	18	19	20	21	22
23/30	24	25	26	27	28	29

HOW TO ESCAPE FROM QUICKSAND

When walking in quicksand country, carry a stout pole—it will help you get out should you need to.

1 As soon as you start to sink, lay the pole on the surface of the quicksand.

2 Do not struggle, and move slowly.
Quicksand is not difficult to float in—but it can suck you down if you struggle too hard against it.

3 Flop onto your back on top of the pole.
After a minute or two, equilibrium in the quicksand will be achieved, and you will no longer sink.

4 Work the pole to a new position: under your hips, and at a right angle to your spine.
The pole will keep your hips from sinking, as you (slowly) pull out first one leg, and then the other.

5 Take the shortest route to firmer ground, moving slowly.

When in an area with quicksand, bring a stout pole and use it to put your back into a floating position.

Place the pole at a right angle to your spine to keep your hips afloat.

JUNE

Monday 10 *New Moon* ●	Tuesday 11	Wednesday 12
		1897—The Swiss Army Knife is legally registered. 1981—*Raiders of the Lost Ark* premieres in theaters.
1909—The first emergency SOS signal is broadcast via telegraph.	1910—Jacques Cousteau is born.	

Thursday 13	Friday 14	Saturday 15
		1752—Benjamin Franklin flies his kite and discovers electricity in lightning.
		Sunday 16
	Flag Day 1775—U.S. Army officially established by Congress.	**Father's Day**

★ **Tip of the Week:**

Floating on quicksand is relatively easy and is the best way to avoid its clutches. You are more buoyant in quicksand than you are in water. If you do not have a pole, spread your arms and legs far apart and try to float on your back.

June

S	M	T	W	T	F	S
						1
2	3	4	5	6	7	8
9	10	11	12	13	14	15
16	17	18	19	20	21	22
23/30	24	25	26	27	28	29

HOW TO FEND OFF
A SHARK

1 Hit back.
If a shark is coming toward you or attacks you, use anything you have in your possession—a camera, probe, harpoon gun, your fist—to hit the shark's eyes or gills, which are the areas most sensitive to pain.

2 Make quick, sharp, repeated jabs in these areas.
Sharks are predators and will usually only follow through on an attack if they have the advantage, so making the shark unsure of its advantage in any way possible will increase your chances of survival. Contrary to popular opinion, the shark's nose is not the area to attack, unless you cannot reach the eyes or gills. Hitting the shark simply tells it that you are not defenseless.

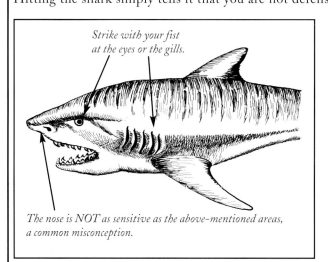

Strike with your fist at the eyes or the gills.

The nose is NOT as sensitive as the above-mentioned areas, a common misconception.

JUNE

Monday *First Quarter* ☾	Tuesday	Wednesday
17	**18**	**19**
1928—Amelia Earhart successfully flies across the Atlantic Ocean.		
Thursday	Friday	Saturday
20	**21**	**22**
		Sunday
		23
1874—First U.S. lifesaving medal is awarded. 1975—*Jaws* premieres in theaters.	Summer Solstice 1958—"Splish Splash" is recorded by Bobby Darin.	

★ Tips of the Week:

- Sharks are more likely to attack an individual, so always stay in groups.
- Avoid being in the water during darkness or twilight hours when sharks are most active and have a competitive sensory advantage.
- Do not enter the water if you are bleeding from an open wound or if you are menstruating; a shark is drawn to blood and its olfactory ability is acute.
- Do not wear shiny jewelry; the reflected light resembles the sheen of fish scales.

June

S	M	T	W	T	F	S
						1
2	3	4	5	6	7	8
9	10	11	12	13	14	15
16	17	18	19	20	21	22
23/30	24	25	26	27	28	29

HOW TO ESCAPE FROM A SINKING CAR

1 Open the window as soon as possible. If you have the presence of mind to get the window open before you hit the water, do it. This is your best chance of escape—opening the door will be very difficult due to the outside water pressure. Opening the window allows water to come in and equalize the pressure. Once the water pressure inside and outside the car is equal, you will be able to open the door or even swim out the window.

As soon as you hit the water, open your window. Otherwise, the pressure of the water will make it very difficult to escape.

If you were unable to open the window before hitting the water, attempt to break it with your foot or a heavy object.

2 If your power windows will not work or you cannot roll your windows down all the way, attempt to break the glass. Use your foot or shoulder, a screwdriver, or a heavy object.

3 Get out as soon as you can.
Do not worry about leaving anything behind unless it is another person. Vehicles with the engine in front will sink at a steep angle, and if the water is 15 feet or deeper, the vehicle may end up on its roof, upside down. Depending on the vehicle, floating time will range from a few seconds to a few minutes. The more airtight the car, the longer it floats.

4 If you are unable to open the window or break it, wait until the car fills with water.
Remain calm and do not panic. When the water level reaches your head, take a deep breath and hold it. Now the pressure should be equalized inside and outside, and you should be able to open the door and swim to the surface.

JUNE

Monday *Full Moon* ○	Tuesday	Wednesday
24	**25**	**26**

Thursday	Friday	Saturday
27	**28**	**29**

Sunday
30

1956—President Eisenhower creates a national highway system.

1953—First Corvette is produced.

★ **Tip of the Week:**

If you are driving your car on a frozen lake, carry several large nails and a length of rope with you. In the event that your car breaks through the ice, the nails will help you pull yourself out of the ice and the rope can be thrown to someone on more solid ground.

June

S	M	T	W	T	F	S
						1
2	3	4	5	6	7	8
9	10	11	12	13	14	15
16	17	18	19	20	21	22
23/30	24	25	26	27	28	29

TRAVELING IN DANGEROUS REGIONS

- **CHECK BEFOREHAND**—When traveling to dangerous parts of the world, always check with authorities beforehand. The U.S. State Department posts warnings on their Web site.
- **I.D. PICTURES**—If you are traveling with friends, spouses, or children, make sure you all have color pictures of each other in case something happens. Carry a photocopy of your passport identification page and a copy of your credit card numbers in a safe hiding place.
- **DRESS**—Dress conservatively, and do not wear or carry obvious signs of wealth.
- **PHOTOS**—Ask permission before taking pictures; do not insist on or sneak photos. Do not take photographs of women, the infirm, or the elderly; doing so may be perceived as intrusive or insulting.
- **AVOID MUGGINGS**—Carry a "mugger's wallet" with you that contains a small amount of money along with a photo ID (not your driver's license or passport) and additional, but replaceable cards, for bulk. Use this wallet for your daily small expenses, but be prepared to surrender it in an emergency.

JULY

Monday	Tuesday *Last Quarter* ☽	Wednesday
1	**2**	**3**

Canada Day

1937—First air raid shelter is built in Idaho.

Thursday	Friday	Saturday
4	**5**	**6**

1886—The first rabies shot is given by Louis Pasteur.

Sunday
7

1891—Traveler's checks are patented by American Express.

Independence Day

1776—The Declaration of Independence is signed.

2000—First appearance of Africanized or killer honeybees in Virginia.

1923—University of Delaware is first in U.S. to establish "junior year abroad."

★ **Tip of the Week:**

In many cities, avoiding eye contact with strangers is a safe way to be left alone. However, be aware that in some foreign countries, it is not considered rude to stare at another person; do not misinterpret anyone who may be staring at you.

July

S	M	T	W	T	F	S
	1	2	3	4	5	6
7	8	9	10	11	12	13
14	15	16	17	18	19	20
21	22	23	24	25	26	27
28	29	30	31			

HOW TO DEAL WITH A CHARGING BULL

1 Do not antagonize the bull, and do not move.
Bulls will generally leave humans alone unless they become angry.

2 Look around for an escape route, cover, or high ground.
Running away is not likely to help unless you find an open door, a fence to jump, or another safe haven—bulls can easily outrun humans. If you can reach such a spot, make a run for it.

3 If you cannot escape to safety, remove an article of clothing.
Use this to distract the bull. It does not matter what color or size the clothing is (you can use a coat, shirt, hat—anything). Despite the colors bullfighters traditionally use, bulls do not naturally head for red—they react to and move toward movement, not color.

4 If the bull charges, remain still and then throw the clothing away from you.
The bull should head toward the object you have thrown, and you can escape in the other direction.

If you cannot find safe cover from a charging bull, remove an article of clothing and throw it away from your body. The bull will head toward the moving object.

JULY

Monday
8

Annual Event: The Festival of San Fermín (the Running of the Bulls) takes place all week in Pamplona, Spain.

Tuesday
9

Wednesday
New Moon ●
10

1921—Jake La Motta, the "Raging Bull" is born.

Thursday
11

1798—U.S. Marine Corps created by an act of Congress.

Friday
12

Saturday
13

1898—Guglielmo Marconi patents the radio.

1942—Harrison Ford is born.

Sunday
14

1789—The Bastille prison falls in Paris, France.

★ **Tip of the Week:**

If you encounter a stampede of bulls or cattle, try to determine which way it is headed, and then get out of the way. If you cannot escape, your only option is to run alongside the stampede to avoid getting trampled. Bulls are not like horses, and will not avoid you if you lie down—so keep moving.

July

S	M	T	W	T	F	S
		1	2	3	4	5	6
7	8	9	10	11	12	13
14	15	16	17	18	19	20
21	22	23	24	25	26	27
28	29	30	31			

HOW TO SURVIVE
A PLANE CRASH

1 Make sure that your seat belt is tightly fastened and that your seat back is fully upright.

2 Bend forward with one arm across your knees.

3 Place your pillow in your lap and hold your head against the pillow with your free arm.

4 Push your legs forward and brace for impact by placing your feet or knees against the seat in front of you.
If you are over water, loosen your shirt (and tie) so that your movement is not restricted when you attempt to swim. Be ready for two jolts: when the plane first hits water and when the nose hits water again.

5 After impact, evacuate as quickly as possible.
Do not take anything with you—if you have something you absolutely cannot part with, you should keep it in your pocket and not in your carry-on baggage.

6 Stay low if the plane is on fire.
Follow the exit procedures described in the safety briefing. Illuminated floor lights should indicate the exits: The lights are red where exit rows exist.

JULY

Monday	Tuesday	Wednesday
## 15	## 16 *First Quarter* ☾	## 17

1916—The Boeing Company is founded in Seattle.

1968—Commercial air travel begins between the U.S. and the U.S.S.R.

Thursday	Friday	Saturday
## 18	## 19	## 20

1969—Neil Armstrong sets foot on the moon.

Sunday
21

1921—John Glenn is born.

1899—Ernest Hemingway is born.

★ **Tips of the Week:**
- Select a seat on the aisle, somewhere in the rear half of the cabin—this is the safest part of the plane.
- Request an emergency exit seat so that you can escape quickly.
- Wear long-sleeved shirts and long pants made of natural fibers to put a barrier between you and any potential heat upon a crash.

July

S	M	T	W	T	F	S
	1	2	3	4	5	6
7	8	9	10	11	12	13
14	15	16	17	18	19	20
21	22	23	24	25	26	27
28	29	30	31			

HOW TO PASS A BRIBE IN A FOREIGN COUNTRY

1 If you are hassled by an official, be friendly, but aloof.
Do not show concern or act surly. Remain calm and good-natured.

2 Never blatantly offer a bribe.
If you have misinterpreted the official's intentions, you may get yourself in additional trouble by overtly offering a bribe.

3 If you are accused of an infraction, ask to pay a fine on the spot.
Say that you would rather not deal with the mail or go to another location, citing your fear that the payment will get lost. Mention that you want to make sure the money gets to the proper person.

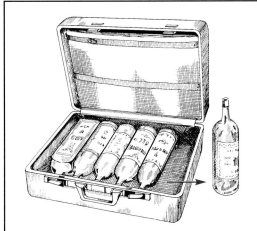

4 Try to speak to and deal with only one official.
Speak to the person who acts as though he or she is in charge. If you offer money to a junior officer while a superior is present, the superior may demand more.

To resolve a customs dispute, you might offer the official a "sample" of the goods in question—for example, a bottle of liquor.

5 Offer to make a "donation" to the official's organization.
Say that you want to pay for gas, uniforms, car repairs, expenses, or other needs.

JULY

Monday	Tuesday	Wednesday	*Full Moon* ○
22	**23**	**24**	
	1888—Raymond Chandler is born.	1898—Amelia Earhart is born.	

Thursday	Friday	Saturday
25	**26**	**27**
		Sunday
		28
	1908—The B.O.I., later renamed the F.B.I., is created.	

★ **Tip of the Week:**

If you don't have cash, offer goods instead. Watches, cameras, and other electronics are often accepted as bribes. If, for example, a customs official tells you that you are transporting too many bottles of liquor, you might speed your trip and lighten your load by offering a bottle to the official.

July

S	M	T	W	T	F	S
		1	2	3	4	5	6
7	8	9	10	11	12	13
14	15	16	17	18	19	20
21	22	23	24	25	26	27
28	29	30	31			

HOW TO SURVIVE IN A PLUMMETING ELEVATOR

Elevators have numerous safety features. There have been very few recorded incidents involving death from plummeting elevators. In general, it is highly unlikely for a cable (also called traction) elevator to fall all the way to the bottom of the shaft. Moreover, the compressed air column in the elevator hoistway and the car buffers at the bottom of the hoistway may keep the forces of the impact survivable.

1 Flatten your body against the car floor.
While there is disagreement among the experts, most recommend this method. This should distribute the force of impact, rather than concentrate it on one area of your body. (Standing may be difficult anyway.)

2 Cover your face and head to protect them from ceiling parts that may break loose.

Lie flat on the floor in the center of the elevator, covering your head for protection.

JULY/AUGUST

Monday **29**	Tuesday **30**	Wednesday **31**
	1947—Arnold Schwarzenegger is born.	

Thursday *Last Quarter* ☽ **1**	Friday **2**	Saturday **3**
		1492—Columbus departs for the New World. 1811—Elisha Graves Otis, inventor of the elevator brake, is born.
		Sunday **4**
1770—William Clark (of Lewis and Clark) is born.		

★ **Tips of the Week:**

- Hydraulic elevators are more likely than cable elevators to fall. Their height is limited to about 70 feet, so a free fall would probably result in injury—but not death.
- Do not jump just before the elevator hits the bottom. The chances that you will jump at exactly the right time are very small. The elevator may collapse around you and crush you if you are still upright in the car.

		July				
S	M	T	W	T	F	S
	1	2	3	4	5	6
7	8	9	10	11	12	13
14	15	16	17	18	19	20
21	22	23	24	25	26	27
28	29	30	31			

		August				
S	M	T	W	T	F	S
					1	2	3
4	5	6	7	8	9	10
11	12	13	14	15	16	17
18	19	20	21	22	23	24
25	26	27	28	29	30	31

HOW TO SURVIVE WHEN YOU FALL THROUGH ICE

1 Turn in the direction from which you came.
You most likely came from the area with the strongest ice.

2 Use your elbows to lift yourself up onto the edge of the hole.
Do not get out yet. Hold yourself up, letting as much water as possible drain from your clothing.

3 Reach out onto the solid ice as far as possible.
If you have a pair of nails, screwdrivers, fisherman ice picks, or car keys, use them to dig into the ice surface to help pull yourself out.

4 Kick your feet as though you were swimming, and pull yourself up as you continue kicking.

5 Once on the ice surface, do not stand up.
Stay flat and roll away from the hole. This distributes your weight more evenly and decreases your chances of breaking through the ice again.

Reach out onto solid ice, digging keys or another item into the ice to help your grip. Kick your feet as you pull yourself out.

AUGUST

Monday **5**	Tuesday **6**	Wednesday **7**
	1926—Gertrude Ederle becomes the first woman to swim the English Channel.	

Thursday **8** *New Moon* ●	Friday **9**	Saturday **10**
		Sunday **11**
	1988—Patent for an ice hole fishing plug is issued.	2000—An 83-year-old woman survives three days in a Florida swamp after her car plunges from a bridge.

★ **Tip of the Week:**

Once you've pulled yourself out of the ice, don't stay in wet clothing for long—get to a shelter as soon as possible and rewarm with dry clothing.

August

S	M	T	W	T	F	S
				1	2	3
4	5	6	7	8	9	10
11	12	13	14	15	16	17
18	19	20	21	22	23	24
25	26	27	28	29	30	31

HOW TO SURVIVE
A SANDSTORM

1 Wet a bandanna or other cloth and place it over your nose and mouth.

Wear a cloth or bandanna over your nose and mouth to avoid inhaling sand particles.

2 Use a small amount of petroleum jelly to coat your nostrils on the inside. The lubricant will help to minimize the drying of mucous membranes.

3 If on foot, all members of your group should stay together.
Link arms or use a rope to avoid becoming separated during the storm and to keep track of group members who might become injured or incapacitated.

4 If driving in a car, pull off the road as far as possible on the shoulder.
Turn off your lights, set the emergency brake, and make sure your taillights are not illuminated. (Vehicles approaching from the rear may inadvertently leave the road and collide with your parked car, thinking it's another vehicle traveling on the road.)

5 Try to move to higher ground.
Sand grains travel across the surface of the earth mostly by saltation, or bouncing from place to place. Because grains of sand will not bounce high on grass, dirt, or sand, moving to solid, high ground is advisable, even if it's just a few feet higher. However, sandstorms can be accompanied by severe thunderstorms, and there may be a risk of lightning. If you hear thunder or see lightning during a sandstorm, do not move to higher ground.

AUGUST

Monday	Tuesday	Wednesday
12	**13**	**14**

Thursday *First Quarter* ☾	Friday	Saturday
15	**16**	**17**

Sunday

18

1620—The *Mayflower* sets sail.

1888—T. E. Lawrence, Lawrence of Arabia, is born.

1896—Klondike Gold Day in the Yukon.

1774—Meriwether Lewis (of Lewis and Clark) is born.

1896—Davy Crockett is born.

★**Tip of the Week:**

Whenever you are in an area with sandstorm potential (anywhere that there is a lot of sand and wind), wear long pants, socks, and shoes. Because of the way sand moves, your feet and lower legs are more likely to be "burned" by the abrasion of sand than the upper part of your body.

August

S	M	T	W	T	F	S
				1	2	3
4	5	6	7	8	9	10
11	12	13	14	15	16	17
18	19	20	21	22	23	24
25	26	27	28	29	30	31

HOW TO MAKE A RAFT

You will need two ponchos or tarps, fresh green brush (enough to cover your poncho or tarp), two fresh saplings (long enough to cross the poncho or tarp in an X, one to two inches in diameter), and rope or vines.

1 Tie off the necks of the ponchos with the neck strings.
Tie rope or vines through the side grommets in the ponchos or tarps. They will need to be long enough to cross and tie with the ropes and vines in the opposite corners.

2 Spread one poncho (tied-off hood up) or tarp on the ground. Pile fresh green brush on the poncho or tarp 18 inches high all around.
Make sure the string from the neck comes through the brush pile.

3 Make an X-frame with the saplings and place it on top of the brush pile. Tie it securely to the brush using the neck rope of the poncho or rope/vines. Pile another 18 inches of brush on the X-frame. Compress the brush.

4 Pull the sides of the poncho/tarp around the pile using the rope/vines, pulling and tying diagonally.

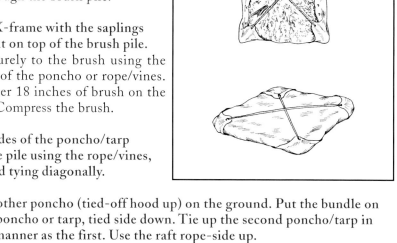

5 Place the other poncho (tied-off hood up) on the ground. Put the bundle on the other poncho or tarp, tied side down. Tie up the second poncho/tarp in the same manner as the first. Use the raft rope-side up.

AUGUST

Monday **19**	Tuesday **20**	Wednesday **21**
		1912—The first Eagle Scout, Arthur R. Eldred, is awarded the highest rank in the Boy Scouts.

Thursday **22** *Full Moon* ○	Friday **23**	Saturday **24**
		79 C.E.—Mt. Vesuvius erupts on Pompeii. 1992—Hurricane Andrew hits the coast of Florida, devastating Miami.
		Sunday **25**
		1930—Sean Connery is born.

★ **Tip of the Week:**

Water is the key to jungle navigation and usually the quickest way to travel, so a raft is essential. Do not travel on rivers at night, however: Alligators and crocodiles are generally night hunters.

August

S	M	T	W	T	F	S
				1	2	3
4	5	6	7	8	9	10
11	12	13	14	15	16	17
18	19	20	21	22	23	24
25	26	27	28	29	30	31

HOW TO ESCAPE FROM KILLER BEES

1 If bees begin flying around and/or stinging you, do not freeze. Run away; swatting at the bees only makes them angrier.

2 Get inside as fast as you can.

3 If no shelter is available, run through bushes or high weeds. This will help give you cover.

4 If a bee stings you, it will leave its stinger in your skin. Remove the stinger by raking your fingernail across it in a sideways motion. Do not pinch or pull the stinger out—this may squeeze more venom from the stinger into your body. Do not let stingers remain in the skin, because venom can continue to pump into the body for up to 10 minutes.

5 Do not jump into a swimming pool or other body of water: the bees are likely to be waiting for you when you surface.

If bees begin flying around and/or stinging you, do not freeze. Do not swat them. Run away. If no shelter is available, run through bushes or high weeds.

AUGUST/SEPTEMBER

Monday	Tuesday	Wednesday
26	**27**	**28**

Thursday	Friday *Last Quarter* ☽	Saturday
29	**30**	**31**

1922—Federal Honeybee Act is enacted to prevent the introduction and spread of diseases harmful to honeybees.

Sunday

1

National Honey Month begins.

★ **Tip of the Week:**

While any colony of bees will defend its hive, Africanized bees do so with gusto. These bees can kill, and they present a danger even to those who are not allergic to bee stings. Regular honeybees will chase you about 50 yards. Africanized honeybees may pursue you three times that distance.

August						
S	M	T	W	T	F	S
				1	2	3
4	5	6	7	8	9	10
11	12	13	14	15	16	17
18	19	20	21	22	23	24
25	26	27	28	29	30	31

September						
S	M	T	W	T	F	S
1	2	3	4	5	6	7
8	9	10	11	12	13	14
15	16	17	18	19	20	21
22	23	24	25	26	27	28
29	30					

HOW TO SURVIVE
ADRIFT AT SEA

1 Stay aboard your boat as long as possible before you get into a life raft.
In a maritime emergency, the rule of thumb is that you should step up into your raft, meaning you should be up to your waist in water before you get into the raft. Your best chance of survival is on a boat, even a disabled one, not in a life raft.

2 Get in the life raft, and take whatever supplies you can.
Most importantly, if you have water in jugs, take it with you. If you must, throw the jugs of water overboard and tie them to the raft so that you can get them later—they will float. Many canned foods, particularly vegetables, are packed in water, so take them with you if you can.

3 Protect yourself from the elements.
If you are in a cold water/weather environment, get warm. If you can provide yourself with some cover from the sun, do so. You are more likely to die of exposure or hypothermia than of anything else.

4 Put on dry clothes if possible and stay out of the water.
Prolonged exposure to saltwater can damage your skin and cause lesions, which are prone to infection.

5 Find food, if you can.
Life rafts include fishing hooks in their survival kits. If your raft is floating for several weeks, seaweed will form on its underside and fish will naturally congregate in the shade under you. You can catch them with the hook and eat the flesh raw. If no hook is available, you can fashion one using wire or even shards of aluminum from an empty can.

6 Try to get to land, if you know where it is.
Most rafts include small paddles. However, life rafts are not very maneuverable, especially in any wind above three knots. Do not exhaust yourself.

SEPTEMBER

Monday
2

Labor Day

1944—George Bush ejects from a burning plane over Japan; after four hours at sea in an inflated raft, he is rescued.

1945—V-J Day

Tuesday
3

Wednesday
4

1965—"Help" by the Beatles goes to #1 on *Billboard*'s Top 40.

Thursday
5

Friday   *New Moon* ●
6

Saturday
7

Rosh Hashanah

Sunday
8

★ **Tip of the Week:**

Do not ration water: Drink it as needed, but do not drink more than is necessary—a half-gallon a day should be sufficient if you limit your activity.

September

S	M	T	W	T	F	S
1	2	3	4	5	6	7
8	9	10	11	12	13	14
15	16	17	18	19	20	21
22	23	24	25	26	27	28
29	30					

HOW TO RAM YOUR CAR THROUGH A BARRICADE

1 Identify the barricade's weakest point.
The side of the barricade that opens, or the place where a lock holds it closed, is usually its most vulnerable spot.

2 Aim for the weak spot.
If possible, use the rear of the car to ram the weak spot—hitting with the front may damage the engine and cause the car to stall.

3 Step on the gas and accelerate to a speed of 30 to 45 mph.
Traveling any faster will cause unnecessary damage to the car. Keep your foot on the gas all the way through. Consider how much room you will need to turn or stop once you clear the barricade.

4 Duck just before impact if you are heading toward an extremely tall barricade or fence.
Pieces of the barricade may break through the window.

5 Avoid poles or anchors in the ground.
These may bend and not break, and then drag against and damage the underside of the car, preventing you from driving.

6 Repeat as necessary to break through.

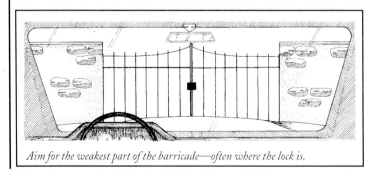

Aim for the weakest part of the barricade—often where the lock is.

SEPTEMBER

Monday
9

1966—Lyndon B. Johnson signs the National Motor Vehicle Safety Act.

Tuesday
10

1913—Lincoln Highway opens as the first coast-to-coast highway.

Wednesday
11

Thursday
12

1978—The TV show *Taxi* premieres on ABC.

Friday   *First Quarter* ☾
13

Saturday
14

Sunday
15

★ **Tip of the Week:**

For electrically-powered gates that swing open and closed (like those found in gated communities and apartment complexes), it is better to push the gate open than to ram it. If you are traveling in the direction the gate opens, simply ease your bumper up to and against the gate. Your car will easily overpower the small electric motor that operates the gate.

September

S	M	T	W	T	F	S
	1	2	3	4	5	6	7
8	9	10	11	12	13	14
15	16	17	18	19	20	21
22	23	24	25	26	27	28
29	30					

HOW TO DEAL WITH A UFO SIGHTING OR ABDUCTION

1   Accurately record the time at the start of the sighting, the time of any change in direction, and the time at the end of the sighting.

2   Try to identify any horizon landmarks with regard to the UFO's position.

3   If you have a video or still camera, record the sighting.
It is essential that the images include some sort of reference information such as a tree, mountain, or skyline.

4   Report the sighting as soon as possible.
Contact the UFO Reporting and Information Service (206-721-5035), the Mutual UFO Network (830-379-2166), or the National UFO Reporting Center (206-722-3000).

IF YOU ARE ATTACKED OR ABDUCTED

1   Resist verbally.
Firmly tell the extraterrestrial biological entity (EBE) to leave you alone.

2   Resist mentally.
Picture yourself enveloped in a protective shield of white light, or in a safe place.

3   Resist physically.
Go for the EBE's eyes—you will not know what its other sensitive areas are.

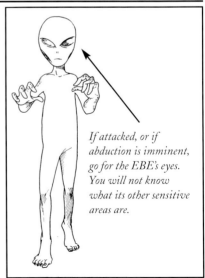

If attacked, or if abduction is imminent, go for the EBE's eyes. You will not know what its other sensitive areas are.

SEPTEMBER

Monday **16**	Tuesday **17**	Wednesday **18**
	1967—The TV show *Mission: Impossible* premieres on CBS.	
Yom Kippur		

Thursday **19**	Friday **20**	Saturday **21** *Full Moon* ○
		Sunday **22**
		Autumnal Equinox
1911—William Golding, author of *Lord of the Flies*, is born.		
1961—Barney and Betty Hill of New Hampshire are reportedly abducted by aliens, one of the first of such incidents.	1519—Ferdinand Magellan sets out on his voyage to circumnavigate the globe.	1921—The Band-Aid is officially registered with the U.S. Patent Office.

★ **Tip of the Week:**

If you are looking for UFOs, keep in mind that most sightings occur in rural areas, away from bright lights, and near military installations. Most sightings occur during the summer months, around 9:00 P.M., with a secondary peak at around 3:00 A.M.

September

S	M	T	W	T	F	S
1	2	3	4	5	6	7
8	9	10	11	12	13	14
15	16	17	18	19	20	21
22	23	24	25	26	27	28
29	30					

HOW TO PURIFY WATER

1 | Filter the water.
This is always the first step to having clean, drinkable water.
- Pour the water through a coffee filter, paper towel, ordinary typing paper, or even your clothing (the more tightly woven, the better). You can also make an effective filter by filling a sock with alternating layers of crushed charcoal, small crushed rocks, and sand.
- Repeat several times.

2 | Chemically treat the water, if available.
Add two drops of household bleach for each quart of water. (Use three drops if the water is extremely cold or cloudy.) If no household bleach is available, use one iodine tablet or five drops of drugstore iodine (2%) per quart of water. Let the mixture sit for at least one hour, to give the chemicals time to kill micro-organisms.

3 | Boil the water.
Boil water for at least one minute, plus one minute of boiling time for each 1,000 feet above sea level you are. If fuel is abundant, boil water for 10 minutes before drinking it. The longer the water boils, the more microorganisms are killed. Beyond 10 minutes, however, no further purification occurs. Be sure to let the water cool before drinking it.

SEPTEMBER

Monday **23**	Tuesday **24**	Wednesday **25**
	1853—Cornelius Vanderbilt begins the first successful around-the-world journey by yacht.	

Thursday **26**	Friday **27**	Saturday **28**
		Sunday *Last Quarter* ☽ **29**
1908—Boontown reservoir opens to supply Jersey City, NJ, with the first chlorine-treated water in the U.S.		

★ **Tip of the Week:**

When purifying water, if you can perform at least one of the recommended steps, you're better off than performing none of them. Remember that the more times you filter the water, the longer it is chemically treated, and the longer you boil it, the purer it will be.

September

S	M	T	W	T	F	S
1	2	3	4	5	6	7
8	9	10	11	12	13	14
15	16	17	18	19	20	21
22	23	24	25	26	27	28
29	30					

HOW TO CONTROL
A RUNAWAY CAMEL

1 Hang on to the reins—do not pull hard in an attempt to stop the camel.
Camels are usually harnessed with a head halter or nose reins, and pulling on the
nose reins can tear the camel's nose—or break the reins.

2 If the camel has sturdy reins and a head halter, pull the reins to one side to
make the camel run in a circle.
Do not fight the camel; pull the reins in the direction the camel is attempting to
turn its head. The camel may change direction several times during the inci-
dent—let it do so. If the camel has nose reins, just hang on tightly, using your
legs to hold on and the reins for balance.

3 Hold on until the camel stops.
Whether the camel is running in circles or straight, it will not run very far. The
camel will sit when it grows tired.

4 When the camel sits, jump off.
Keep hold of the reins to keep it from running away.

*Hang on tight and
pull the reins to one side
to make the camel run
in a circle. It will stop
on its own.*

SEPTEMBER/OCTOBER

Monday
30

1627—Daniel DeFoe's character, Robinson Crusoe, is "born."

Tuesday
1

Wednesday
2

1721—The first camel is brought to the U.S. to be exhibited in Boston.

Thursday
3

Friday
4

1957—*Sputnik 1* is launched by the U.S.S.R.

Saturday
5

Sunday   *New Moon* ●
6

★ **Tip of the Week:**

Always remember that camels are basically lazy animals and will not run for long (usually no more than a few minutes).

September

S	M	T	W	T	F	S
1	2	3	4	5	6	7
8	9	10	11	12	13	14
15	16	17	18	19	20	21
22	23	24	25	26	27	28
29	30					

October

S	M	T	W	T	F	S
			1	2	3	4	5
6	7	8	9	10	11	12
13	14	15	16	17	18	19
20	21	22	23	24	25	26
27	28	29	30	31		

HOW TO JUMP FROM ROOF TO ROOF

1 If you have time, look for any obstructions at the ledge.
You may have to clear short walls, gutters, or other obstacles as well as the space between buildings.

2 Check your target building.
Make certain that you have enough space to land and roll. If the target building is lower than your building, assess how much lower it is. You risk broken ankles or legs if there is more than a one story differential in the buildings. Two stories or more and you risk a broken back.

3 Check the distance between the buildings.
Most people cannot jump further than 10 feet, even at a full run. If the buildings are further apart than this distance, you risk catastrophic injury or death. You could successfully leap a span across an alley, but not a two-lane road.

4 Pick a spot for take-off and a spot for landing.

5 Run at full speed toward the edge.
You must be running as fast as you can to attempt a leap of a distance of more than a few feet. You will need 40 to 60 feet to gain enough speed to clear about 10 feet of distance.

6 Leap.
Make sure your center of gravity is over the edge of your target building in case your whole body doesn't clear the span and you have to grab hold. Jump with your arms and hands extended and ready to grab the ledge if necessary.

7 Try to land on your feet, then immediately tuck your head and tumble sideways onto your shoulders, not forward onto your head.

OCTOBER

Monday **7**	Tuesday **8**	Wednesday **9**
		1984—Kathy Sullivan becomes the first woman to walk in outer space.

Thursday **10**	Friday **11**	Saturday **12** *First Quarter* ☾
		Columbus Day 1975—Marian Jones, Olympic long jumper, is born.
		Sunday **13**
	1871—The Chicago Fire is finally put out after burning for three days.	

★ **Tip of the Week:**

It is nearly impossible to leap to a building that is more than one story higher than the one you are on. Seek an alternate escape if all the surrounding buildings are taller.

October

S	M	T	W	T	F	S
		1	2	3	4	5
6	7	8	9	10	11	12
13	14	15	16	17	18	19
20	21	22	23	24	25	26
27	28	29	30	31		

HOW TO CLIMB
OUT OF A WELL

This method is known as the Chimney Climbing Technique.

1 Place your back against one wall and your feet against the other wall.
Your body will be in an "L" shape, with your back straight, your legs sticking out, and the soles of your feet pressing against the opposite wall. If the well is tilted in one direction, place your back on the lower wall.

2 Use even, steady pressure from your thighs to maintain traction on your feet and friction on your back, and to hold yourself off the ground.

3 Place the palms of your hands against the wall behind you, below your buttocks.

4 Take your right foot off the opposite wall and place it under your backside.

5 While pressing your back away from the wall with your hands, push up with your hands and your feet.
Move only about 6 to 10 inches.

6 Place your back on the wall again and move your right foot back onto the opposite wall, a bit higher than your left foot.

7 Repeat the procedure, beginning with your left foot.
Alternate feet, slowly working your way to the lip of the well, resting each time.

8 When you approach the lip of the well, reach up with your hand overhead and perform a "mantle move."
Pull yourself halfway up from a chin-up hang position, then roll (shift) your weight onto your forearms as they clear the lip of the well. Shift your body weight to your hands, and press up. Use your feet against the wall to assist in pulling yourself up out of the well.

OCTOBER

Monday	Tuesday	Wednesday
14	**15**	**16**
Columbus Day Observed Canadian Thanksgiving		1987—Baby Jessica McClure is rescued from a well in Midland, TX.

Thursday	Friday	Saturday
17	**18**	**19**
		Sunday **20**
1938—Evel Knievel is born.	1968—U.S. athlete Bob Beamon sets the long jump record (29 feet, 2 inches).	1911—Roald Amundsen sets out for the South Pole.

★ **Tip of the Week:**

Use the Chimney Climbing Technique when the opening is narrow enough to keep your back against one wall and your feet against the opposite side.

October

S	M	T	W	T	F	S
		1	2	3	4	5
6	7	8	9	10	11	12
13	14	15	16	17	18	19
20	21	22	23	24	25	26
27	28	29	30	31		

HOW TO SURVIVE
A TRIP OVER A WATERFALL

1 Take a deep breath just before going over the edge.
You probably will not have much control while you are in the air, and you may be held under water at the bottom.

2 Go over the falls feet first.
The biggest danger in going over a waterfall is hitting your head on something underwater and being knocked unconscious. There is still a risk of broken limbs.

3 Jump straight out and away from the edge of the falls just before you go over.
Cover your head with your arms.

4 Start swimming immediately upon hitting the water, even before you surface.
Swimming will slow your descent.

Jump away from the edge and go over the falls feet first, covering your head.

5 Swim downstream, away from the falls.
It is essential that you avoid being trapped behind the waterfall or on the rocks underneath.

OCTOBER

Monday *Full Moon* ○	Tuesday	Wednesday
21	**22**	**23**

1989—Buck Helm is found alive after being buried for four days by an earthquake in San Francisco.

Thursday	Friday	Saturday
24	**25**	**26**

Sunday
27

United Nations Day

1901—The first person jumps over Niagara Falls in a barrel.

1945—The United Nations is officially established.

★ **Tip of the Week:**

At the base of the falls, the water recirculates, and may pull you under. If this happens, swim to the bottom, then over to shore underwater.

October

S	M	T	W	T	F	S
		1	2	3	4	5
6	7	8	9	10	11	12
13	14	15	16	17	18	19
20	21	22	23	24	25	26
27	28	29	30	31		

HOW TO DEAL WITH A DOWNED POWER LINE

1 Stay far away from downed lines. Current can travel through any conductive material; beware of water on the ground. Direct contact is not necessary for electrocution to occur—simply interacting with the particles near the charged wire may be enough to produce an electric spark.

2 Do not assume that a non-sparking wire is safe. Power may have been restored by automated equipment, causing a "dead" wire to become dangerous.

Never touch a vehicle that has come into contact with a live wire. Even when the wire is removed, it may retain a charge.

Do not assume that a nonsparking wire is safe.

Current can travel through any conductive material such as water.

3 If a person comes into contact with a live wire, use a nonconductive material to separate the person from the electrical source. Use a wooden broom handle, a wooden chair, or a dry towel or sheet. Rubber or insulated gloves offer no protection.

4 Avoid direct contact with the skin or conductive clothing of the victim until he or she is disconnected; you may be shocked also.

5 Check the pulse and begin rescue breathing and CPR if necessary.

OCTOBER/NOVEMBER

Monday *Last Quarter* ☽	Tuesday	Wednesday
28	**29**	**30**

1929—The first recorded birth of a baby in an airplane.

Thursday	Friday	Saturday
31	**1**	**2**

1734—Daniel Boone is born.

1785—The first lifeboat is patented.

Sunday
3

Halloween

1860—Juliette Gordon Law, the founder of the Girl Scouts of America, is born.

1931—Synthetic rubber is first manufactured.

★ **Tip of the Week:**

If you are in a car and a pole or power line falls nearby, it is safer to stay in the vehicle than to attempt to get out of it—the metal cage of the car offers enough protection. If the wire falls onto the car, do not touch any metal in the car, and stay put until help arrives.

October

S	M	T	W	T	F	S
		1	2	3	4	5
6	7	8	9	10	11	12
13	14	15	16	17	18	19
20	21	22	23	24	25	26
27	28	29	30	31		

November

S	M	T	W	T	F	S
					1	2
3	4	5	6	7	8	9
10	11	12	13	14	15	16
17	18	19	20	21	22	23
24	25	26	27	28	29	30

THE LEWIS AND CLARK EXPEDITION

In May 1804, Meriwether Lewis and William Clark embarked on a two-year, 8,000-mile journey with a team called the "Corps of Discovery." The 33 men traveled from St. Louis, Missouri, to the Pacific coast of Oregon and back. It was the first exploration launched by the U.S. government, embarking after President Thomas Jefferson had acquired the Louisiana Purchase.

The mission was threefold: 1) Find the Northwest Passage, a waterway between the Atlantic and Pacific; 2) Announce American sovereignty to the native peoples and foreign interests already inhabiting the territory; and 3) Document in detail the flora and fauna of the unknown landscape.

The group traveled north up the Missouri River on their way to North Dakota, where they set up camp for the winter. When reembarking in April 1805, Sacajawea joined the team and was invaluable as an interpreter and negotiator, helping secure horses and supplies for the group along the way.

The seven-month journey to the Pacific was treacherous. The expedition labored in deep snow through Montana before reaching the Snake and Columbia Rivers, which would carry them to the coast of Oregon on November 8, 1805. They rested there for the rest of the winter.

The group split up for the trip home, but all made it back to St. Louis safely. These explorers survived unimaginable hardships to chart our great country.

NOVEMBER

Monday
New Moon ●
4

1846—B. F. Palmer obtains the patent for an artificial leg.

Tuesday
5

Election Day

Wednesday
6

Thursday
7

Friday
8

1805—Lewis and Clark reach the Pacific Ocean.

Saturday
9

Sunday
10

★ **Tip of the Week:**

When traveling in unknown or foreign places, always enlist the help of trusted natives. You will likely have to pay for their services, but in a potentially dangerous region, it is always worth it.

November

S	M	T	W	T	F	S
					1	2
3	4	5	6	7	8	9
10	11	12	13	14	15	16
17	18	19	20	21	22	23
24	25	26	27	28	29	30

HOW TO STOP A CAR
WITH FAILED BRAKES

1 Begin pumping the brake pedal and keep pumping it.
You may be able to build up enough pressure in the braking system to slow down a bit, or even stop completely. If you have anti-lock brakes, you do not normally pump them—but if your brakes have failed, this may work.

2 Shift the car into the lowest gear possible and let the engine and transmission slow you down.

3 Pull the emergency brake—but not too hard.
Pulling too hard on the emergency brake (also known as the hand brake or parking brake) will cause the rear wheels to lock, and the car to spin around. Use even, constant pressure. In most cars, the emergency brake is cable operated and serves as a fail-safe brake that should work even when the rest of the braking system has failed. The car should slow down and, in combination with the lower gear, will eventually stop.

4 If you have room, swerve the car back and forth across the road.
Making hard turns at each side of the road will decrease your speed even more.

5 If you come up behind another car, use it to help you stop.
Blow your horn, flash your lights, and try to get the driver's attention. If you hit the car, hit it square, bumper to bumper, so you do not knock the other car off the road. This is an extremely dangerous maneuver: It works best if the vehicle in front of you is larger than yours—a bus or truck is ideal—and if both vehicles are traveling at similar speeds. You do not want to crash into a much slower-moving or stopped vehicle, however.

6 Look for something to help stop you.
A flat or uphill road that intersects with the road you are on, a field, or a fence will slow you further but not stop you suddenly. Avoid trees and wooden telephone poles; they do not yield as readily. Do not attempt to sideswipe oncoming cars, but other large objects could help you come to a stop.

NOVEMBER

Monday *First Quarter* ☾	Tuesday	Wednesday
11	**12**	**13**
Veterans Day Remembrance Day (Canada)		

Thursday	Friday	Saturday
14	**15**	**16**
		1901—An automobile exceeds the speed of one mile per minute (60 mph) for the first time.
		Sunday **17**
	1965—Craig Breedlove, inventor of the jet-car, sets the land speed record (600 mph).	

★ **Tip of the Week:**

If you are quickly running out of room and other methods are unsuccessful, try a "bootlegger's turn." Yank the emergency brake hard while turning the wheel a quarter turn. This will spin the car 180 degrees. If you were heading downhill, this spin will head you back uphill, allowing you to slow down.

November

S	M	T	W	T	F	S
					1	2
3	4	5	6	7	8	9
10	11	12	13	14	15	16
17	18	19	20	21	22	23
24	25	26	27	28	29	30

HOW TO TREAT A SCORPION STING

Most species of scorpion have venom of low to moderate toxicity and do not pose a serious health threat to adult humans, other than severe pain.

1 Apply heat or cold packs to the sting site for pain relief.
The most severe pain usually occurs at the site of the sting. Also use an analgesic (painkiller) if available.

2 If an allergic reaction occurs, take an antihistamine.
Scorpion venom contains histamines, which may cause allergic reactions (asthma, rashes) in sensitive persons.

3 Watch for an irregular heartbeat, tingling in extremities, an inability to move limbs or fingers, or difficulty breathing.
Most scorpion stings cause only instantaneous pain at the site of the sting. The pain may radiate over the body several minutes after the initial sting. Pain tends to be felt in joints, especially in the armpits and groin. Systemic symptoms may also occur—possibly numbness in the face, mouth, or throat; muscle twitches; sweating; nausea; vomiting; fever; and restlessness. These symptoms are normal and not life-threatening, and usually subside in one to three hours. The site of the sting may remain sore for one to three days.

4 Seek emergency medical care if you exhibit the above symptoms. An adult will survive even if it takes 12 hours or more to get to a hospital, but a small child will need medical care immediately.

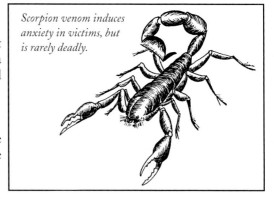

Scorpion venom induces anxiety in victims, but is rarely deadly.

5 Do not apply tourniquets.
The toxins are small and move extremely rapidly away from the site of the sting.

NOVEMBER

Monday **18**	Tuesday **19** *Full Moon* ○	Wednesday **20**
1923—Alan Shepard, astronaut (and Scorpio), is born.		1497—Vasco da Gama rounds Cape of Good Hope, discovering a water route from Europe to India.
Thursday **21**	Friday **22**	Saturday **23**
		Sunday **24**
		1874—Joseph Glidden patents barbed wire.

★ **Tip of the Week:**

If you have been stung by a scorpion, never cut the wound or allow anyone to suck out the poison. This can cause infection or transfer the venom into the bloodstream of the person attempting to remove the poison.

November

S	M	T	W	T	F	S
					1	2
3	4	5	6	7	8	9
10	11	12	13	14	15	16
17	18	19	20	21	22	23
24	25	26	27	28	29	30

HOW TO SAFELY RAM A CAR OUT OF YOUR WAY

1 Fasten your seat belt.

2 Disable your air bag, if you can. It will deploy on impact and obstruct your view.

3 Accelerate to at least 25 mph. Do not go too fast—keeping the car at a slow speed will allow you to maintain control. Just before impact, increase your speed to greater than 30 mph to deliver a disabling crunch to the obstacle car.

4 Ram the front passenger side of your car into the obstacle car at its rear wheel, at a 90 degree angle (the cars should be perpendicular).

5 If you are unable to hit the car in the rear, go for the front right corner. Avoid hitting the car squarely in the side; this will not move it out of your way.

6 The car should spin out of your way—hit the gas, and keep moving.

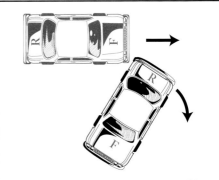

Ram the obstacle car with the passenger side of your car, and deliver a disabling crunch to its rear wheel.

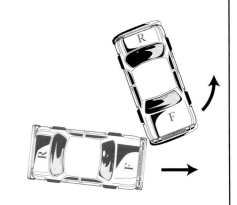

If you are unable to hit the car in the rear, go for the front right corner.

NOVEMBER/DECEMBER

Monday 25	Tuesday 26	Wednesday 27 *Last Quarter* ☽
		1870—Joe Mack, co-founder of Mack Truck Company, is born.

Thursday 28	Friday 29	Saturday 30
		Chanukah 1667—Jonathan Swift, author of *Gulliver's Travels*, is born.
		Sunday 1
Thanksgiving	1929—Richard Byrd completes the first plane flight over the South Pole.	

★ **Tip of the Week:**

No matter how angry or endangered you are, ramming a car to move it out of your way is not easy or safe. However, these methods work better than others, and will minimize the damage to your vehicle.

November

S	M	T	W	T	F	S
					1	2
3	4	5	6	7	8	9
10	11	12	13	14	15	16
17	18	19	20	21	22	23
24	25	26	27	28	29	30

December

S	M	T	W	T	F	S
1	2	3	4	5	6	7
8	9	10	11	12	13	14
15	16	17	18	19	20	21
22	23	24	25	26	27	28
29	30	31				

HOW TO PERFORM
A FAST 180-DEGREE TURN
WITH YOUR CAR

1 While in drive or a forward gear, accelerate to a moderate rate of speed. Anything faster than 45 mph risks flipping the car.

2 Slip the car into neutral to prevent the front wheels from spinning.

3 Take your foot off the gas and turn the wheel 90 degrees (a quarter-turn) while simultaneously pulling hard on the emergency brake.

4 As the rear swings around, return the wheel to its original position and put the car back into drive.

5 Step on the gas to start moving in the direction from which you came.

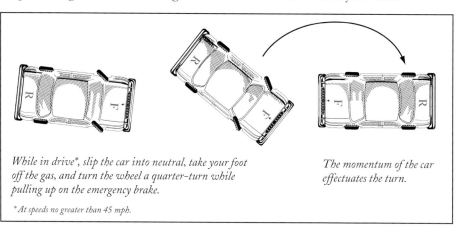

While in drive*, slip the car into neutral, take your foot off the gas, and turn the wheel a quarter-turn while pulling up on the emergency brake.

The momentum of the car effectuates the turn.

* At speeds no greater than 45 mph.

DECEMBER

Monday
2

1927—The first Ford Model A is sold, for $395.

Tuesday
New Moon ●
3

1951—Auto racer Rick Mears is born.

Wednesday
4

Thursday
5

1848—The Gold Rush begins.

Friday
6

Saturday
7

1869—First known bank robbery by the James Gang.

Sunday
8

1861—William Durant, founder of General Motors, is born.

★ **Tip of the Week:**

Road conditions can play a significant role in the success—and safety—of this maneuver. Any surface without sufficient traction (dirt, mud, ice, gravel) will make quick turns harder and collisions more likely.

December

S	M	T	W	T	F	S
1	2	3	4	5	6	7
8	9	10	11	12	13	14
15	16	17	18	19	20	21
22	23	24	25	26	27	28
29	30	31				

HOW TO CROSS
A PIRANHA-INFESTED RIVER

1 Do not cross if you have an open wound.
Piranhas are attracted to blood.

2 Avoid areas with netted fish, docks where fish are cleaned, and areas around bird rookeries.
Piranhas may become habituated to feeding in these areas and may be more aggressive there.

3 Stay out of the water when piranhas are feeding.
When large numbers of piranhas are attacking prey—a true feeding frenzy—they may snap and bite at anything around them. If you see them feeding, stay away, or well upriver.

4 Cross the river at night.
Virtually every species of piranha rests at night, and when awakened, will swim away rather than attack. Piranhas are most active at dawn, though some large adults may hunt in the evening.

5 Swim or walk across quickly and quietly.
Try not to create a large disturbance in the water that might awaken piranhas.

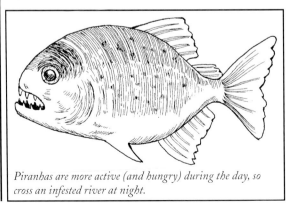

Piranhas are more active (and hungry) during the day, so cross an infested river at night.

DECEMBER

Monday
9

1854—Tennyson's poem "Charge of the Light Brigade" is published.

Tuesday
10

Wednesday
First Quarter ☾
11

1844—Nitrous oxide is first used in a tooth extraction operation in Hartford, CT.

Thursday
12

Friday
13

1577—Sir Francis Drake sets sail from England on a trip around the world.

Saturday
14

1911—Roald Amundsen reaches the South Pole.

Sunday
15

★ **Tip of the Week:**

Piranhas generally do not attack humans or large animals—unless they are already dead or injured. During the dry season, however, when their food supply is scarce, they can be more aggressive.

December

S	M	T	W	T	F	S
	1	2	3	4	5	6	7
8	9	10	11	12	13	14
15	16	17	18	19	20	21
22	23	24	25	26	27	28
29	30	31				

HOW TO DISABLE A CAR

FROM UNDER THE HOOD

1 Use a pry bar to release the safety latch that holds the hood closed.

2 Remove the battery.
This is the easiest method to disable a car—it is often what the police do when they find stolen cars.

FROM INSIDE THE CAR

1 Remove the steering wheel cover by inserting a flat-head screwdriver between the wheel and the cover and prying it off.

2 Remove the ignition (the part the key fits into) with your screwdriver.

3 Cross the red and black wires to short out the ignition.

FROM UNDERNEATH THE CAR

★ Cut the starter wire.
The starter wire is red and on most cars is located on the passenger side.

FROM BEHIND THE CAR

★ Plug up the tailpipe.
Preferably, the object you use should expand slightly once it is inside the pipe. The object must be in the muffler pipe firmly so that it is not expelled when the car is started. This method is also fairly easy to reverse.

DECEMBER

Monday	Tuesday	Wednesday
16	**17**	**18**
	1903—The Wright brothers complete the first successful flight of a mechanically propelled airplane at Kitty Hawk, NC.	

Thursday *Full Moon* ○	Friday	Saturday
19	**20**	**21**
		Winter Solstice
		Sunday
		22
1790—Arctic explorer Sir William Parry is born.	1868—Harvey Firestone, founder of Firestone Tire and Rubber Company, is born.	1937—The Lincoln Tunnel, connecting New Jersey and New York City, opens.

★ **Tip of the Week:**

One of the most effective, non-destructive methods for disabling a car is to simply let the air out of the tires. Use a pressure gauge, pen, stick, or other object to depress and hold down the pin in the center of the tire valve to let the air out.

December

S	M	T	W	T	F	S
1	2	3	4	5	6	7
8	9	10	11	12	13	14
15	16	17	18	19	20	21
22	23	24	25	26	27	28
29	30	31				

HOW TO IDENTIFY AND AVOID MINEFIELDS

There are four basic mine types:

TRIPWIRE MINES—Stepping across a wire attached to the detonator will cause the mine to explode.

DIRECT PRESSURE MINES—Stepping down on a pressure-sensitive pad will activate the detonator.

TIMER MINES—A timer can be an electrical clock, a digital clock, a dripping/mixing chemical, or a mechanical timer that will detonate the mine.

REMOTE MINES—A remote mine can be detonated via an electrical charge across a wire (a "clacker"), via a radio signal, or from a heat or sound sensor.

If you find yourself in a minefield, follow these steps to avoid detonating one.

1 Keep your eyes on your feet.

2 Do not move forward any further.

3 Look for spikes, detonators, wires, or bumps and discoloration in the ground around you.

4 Avoid these areas, and back up slowly in your own footsteps. Do not turn around. Walk backward.

5 Stop when you are certain you are safe.

DECEMBER

Monday	Tuesday	Wednesday
23	**24**	**25**
	1977—"Staying Alive" by the Bee Gees debuts on *Billboard*'s Top 40. 1986—*Platoon* is released in theaters.	Christmas

Thursday *Last Quarter* ☽	Friday	Saturday
26	**27**	**28**
		Sunday **29**
Kwanzaa Boxing Day (Canada)		1800—Charles Goodyear, inventor of the rubber tire, is born.

★ **Tip of the Week:**

When in a region where mines may be, such as a post-war country, look out for:

- Dirt that has been disturbed.
- Wires across trails.
- Newly destroyed vehicles on or just off the road.
- Brush, overgrown fields, and trails.
- Fields of dead animals.

December

S	M	T	W	T	F	S
1	2	3	4	5	6	7
8	9	10	11	12	13	14
15	16	17	18	19	20	21
22	23	24	25	26	27	28
29	30	31				

HOW TO LOSE SOMEONE
WHO IS FOLLOWING YOU

1 | Determine if you are actually being followed.
Make three to four turns in a row to see if the car continues to follow you. Signal a turn in one direction but turn quickly in the other direction. See if the other car turns as well.

2 | Once you are certain you are being followed, get on a highway, or drive to a populous and active area.
Do not drive home, to a deserted place, or down an alley. You are more likely to shake your pursuer in a crowd than in a deserted area.

3 | Drive at the speed limit, or a bit slower.
Soon, another car (not that of your pursuer) will attempt to pass you. Speed up so that the car pulls in behind you. Repeat, but don't go so slowly that an innocent car is able to pass you.

4 | Slow down at a busy intersection with a traffic light, then accelerate through the intersection just after the light changes.
Your pursuer may get stuck at the red light. If you attract the attention of the police for running a red light, your pursuer will most likely leave the scene.

5 | When there are several cars around you, speed up, get off the highway (if you are on one), and make several quick turns to further elude your pursuer.
Your pursuer should be too far back to follow closely.

6 | Once you are out of sight of your pursuer, pull into a parking lot, a garage, or a shopping center with lots of other cars.

7 | If you still have not lost the other car, drive to a police station and get help.

DECEMBER/JANUARY

Monday
30

1940—The first California freeway opens.

Tuesday
31

1984—The nation's first mandatory seatbelt law goes into effect.

Wednesday
1

New Year's Day

Thursday   *New Moon* ●
2

1974—President Nixon sets the national speed limit at 55 mph.

Friday
3

Saturday
4

Sunday
5

★ **Tip of the Week:**

If you can, make note of the license plate of the tailing car, as well as the color, style, and make, and any distinguishing characteristics (front bumper stickers, dents, other decorations).

December						
S	M	T	W	T	F	S
1	2	3	4	5	6	7
8	9	10	11	12	13	14
15	16	17	18	19	20	21
22	23	24	25	26	27	28
29	30	31				

January						
S	M	T	W	T	F	S
				1	2	3	4
5	6	7	8	9	10	11
12	13	14	15	16	17	18
19	20	21	22	23	24	25
26	27	28	29	30	31	

2001

January
S	M	T	W	T	F	S
	1	2	3	4	5	6
7	8	9	10	11	12	13
14	15	16	17	18	19	20
21	22	23	24	25	26	27
28	29	30	31			

February
S	M	T	W	T	F	S
				1	2	3
4	5	6	7	8	9	10
11	12	13	14	15	16	17
18	19	20	21	22	23	24
25	26	27	28			

March
S	M	T	W	T	F	S
				1	2	3
4	5	6	7	8	9	10
11	12	13	14	15	16	17
18	19	20	21	22	23	24
25	26	27	28	29	30	31

April
S	M	T	W	T	F	S
1	2	3	4	5	6	7
8	9	10	11	12	13	14
15	16	17	18	19	20	21
22	23	24	25	26	27	28
29	30					

May
S	M	T	W	T	F	S
		1	2	3	4	5
6	7	8	9	10	11	12
13	14	15	16	17	18	19
20	21	22	23	24	25	26
27	28	29	30	31		

June
S	M	T	W	T	F	S
					1	2
3	4	5	6	7	8	9
10	11	12	13	14	15	16
17	18	19	20	21	22	23
24	25	26	27	28	29	30

July
S	M	T	W	T	F	S
1	2	3	4	5	6	7
8	9	10	11	12	13	14
15	16	17	18	19	20	21
22	23	24	25	26	27	28
29	30	31				

August
S	M	T	W	T	F	S
			1	2	3	4
5	6	7	8	9	10	11
12	13	14	15	16	17	18
19	20	21	22	23	24	25
26	27	28	29	30	31	

September
S	M	T	W	T	F	S
						1
2	3	4	5	6	7	8
9	10	11	12	13	14	15
16	17	18	19	20	21	22
23/30	24	25	26	27	28	29

October
S	M	T	W	T	F	S
	1	2	3	4	5	6
7	8	9	10	11	12	13
14	15	16	17	18	19	20
21	22	23	24	25	26	27
28	29	30	31			

November
S	M	T	W	T	F	S
				1	2	3
4	5	6	7	8	9	10
11	12	13	14	15	16	17
18	19	20	21	22	23	24
25	26	27	28	29	30	

December
S	M	T	W	T	F	S
						1
2	3	4	5	6	7	8
9	10	11	12	13	14	15
16	17	18	19	20	21	22
23/30	24/31	25	26	27	28	29

2002

January

S	M	T	W	T	F	S
		1	2	3	4	5
6	7	8	9	10	11	12
13	14	15	16	17	18	19
20	21	22	23	24	25	26
27	28	29	30	31		

February

S	M	T	W	T	F	S
					1	2
3	4	5	6	7	8	9
10	11	12	13	14	15	16
17	18	19	20	21	22	23
24	25	26	27	28		

March

S	M	T	W	T	F	S
					1	2
3	4	5	6	7	8	9
10	11	12	13	14	15	16
17	18	19	20	21	22	23
24/31	25	26	27	28	29	30

April

S	M	T	W	T	F	S
	1	2	3	4	5	6
7	8	9	10	11	12	13
14	15	16	17	18	19	20
21	22	23	24	25	26	27
28	29	30				

May

S	M	T	W	T	F	S
			1	2	3	4
5	6	7	8	9	10	11
12	13	14	15	16	17	18
19	20	21	22	23	24	25
26	27	28	29	30	31	

June

S	M	T	W	T	F	S
						1
2	3	4	5	6	7	8
9	10	11	12	13	14	15
16	17	18	19	20	21	22
23/30	24	25	26	27	28	29

July

S	M	T	W	T	F	S
	1	2	3	4	5	6
7	8	9	10	11	12	13
14	15	16	17	18	19	20
21	22	23	24	25	26	27
28	29	30	31			

August

S	M	T	W	T	F	S
				1	2	3
4	5	6	7	8	9	10
11	12	13	14	15	16	17
18	19	20	21	22	23	24
25	26	27	28	29	30	31

September

S	M	T	W	T	F	S
1	2	3	4	5	6	7
8	9	10	11	12	13	14
15	16	17	18	19	20	21
22	23	24	25	26	27	28
29	30					

October

S	M	T	W	T	F	S
		1	2	3	4	5
6	7	8	9	10	11	12
13	14	15	16	17	18	19
20	21	22	23	24	25	26
27	28	29	30	31		

November

S	M	T	W	T	F	S
					1	2
3	4	5	6	7	8	9
10	11	12	13	14	15	16
17	18	19	20	21	22	23
24	25	26	27	28	29	30

December

S	M	T	W	T	F	S
1	2	3	4	5	6	7
8	9	10	11	12	13	14
15	16	17	18	19	20	21
22	23	24	25	26	27	28
29	30	31				

2003

January

S	M	T	W	T	F	S
			1	2	3	4
5	6	7	8	9	10	11
12	13	14	15	16	17	18
19	20	21	22	23	24	25
26	27	28	29	30	31	

February

S	M	T	W	T	F	S
						1
2	3	4	5	6	7	8
9	10	11	12	13	14	15
16	17	18	19	20	21	22
23	24	25	26	27	28	

March

S	M	T	W	T	F	S
						1
2	3	4	5	6	7	8
9	10	11	12	13	14	15
16	17	18	19	20	21	22
$^{23}/_{30}$	$^{24}/_{31}$	25	26	27	28	29

April

S	M	T	W	T	F	S
		1	2	3	4	5
6	7	8	9	10	11	12
13	14	15	16	17	18	19
20	21	22	23	24	25	26
27	28	29	30			

May

S	M	T	W	T	F	S
				1	2	3
4	5	6	7	8	9	10
11	12	13	14	15	16	17
18	19	20	21	22	23	24
25	26	27	28	29	30	31

June

S	M	T	W	T	F	S
1	2	3	4	5	6	7
8	9	10	11	12	13	14
15	16	17	18	19	20	21
22	23	24	25	26	27	28
29	30					

July

S	M	T	W	T	F	S
		1	2	3	4	5
6	7	8	9	10	11	12
13	14	15	16	17	18	19
20	21	22	23	24	25	26
27	28	29	30	31		

August

S	M	T	W	T	F	S
					1	2
3	4	5	6	7	8	9
10	11	12	13	14	15	16
17	18	19	20	21	22	23
$^{24}/_{31}$	25	26	27	28	29	30

September

S	M	T	W	T	F	S
	1	2	3	4	5	6
7	8	9	10	11	12	13
14	15	16	17	18	19	20
21	22	23	24	25	26	27
28	29	30				

October

S	M	T	W	T	F	S
			1	2	3	4
5	6	7	8	9	10	11
12	13	14	15	16	17	18
19	20	21	22	23	24	25
26	27	28	29	30	31	

November

S	M	T	W	T	F	S
						1
2	3	4	5	6	7	8
9	10	11	12	13	14	15
16	17	18	19	20	21	22
$^{23}/_{30}$	24	25	26	27	28	29

December

S	M	T	W	T	F	S
	1	2	3	4	5	6
7	8	9	10	11	12	13
14	15	16	17	18	19	20
21	22	23	24	25	26	27
28	29	30	31			

SURVIVAL NOTES

SURVIVAL NOTES

About the Experts

How to Jump from a Bridge or Cliff into a River
Source: Christopher Caso, stuntman, has produced and performed high-fall stunts for numerous movies, including *Batman and Robin*, *The Lost World*, and *The Crow: City of Angels*.

How to Deal with Army Ants
Source: Dr. Bill Gotwald, Professor of Biology at Utica College of Syracuse University, is the author of *Army Ants: The Biology of Social Predation*, which represents the capstone of a thirty-year research career with army ants.

How to Build a Snow Cave
Source: John Lindner, director of the Wilderness Survival School for the Colorado Mountain Club and Director of Training for the Snow Operations Training Center.

How to Escape from Bondage
Sources: Tom Flanagan ("The Amazing Flanagan"), magician and escape artist; *The Book of Survival* by Anthony Greenburg.

How to Build an Animal Trap
Source: Ron Hood, survival expert, received his early wilderness training while a member of the U.S. Army and taught wilderness survival classes for 20 years. Currently, he and his wife Karen produce wilderness survival training videos.

How to Survive in Frigid Water
Source: Tim Smalley is a Boating and Water Safety Education Coordinator for the Minnesota Department of Natural Resources.

How to Fool a Lie Detector Test
Source: James F. Masucci, a police officer for 17 years and detective for 12, is the owner of TCB Investigations & Consultant, a private investigation and security consulting business. He is a certified Voice Stress Analyst.

How to Survive in Whitewater Rapids after Falling out of Your Raft
Sources: Jon Turk, author of *Cold Oceans: Adventures in Kayak, Rowboat, and Dogsled*; www.coldoceans.com; Christopher Macarak, kayak instructor, owner of Paddle Trax Kayak Shop in Crested Butte, Colorado.

How to Escape from a Car Hanging Over the Edge of a Cliff
Source: Christopher Caso.

How to Take a Punch
Source: Cappy Kotz is a USA Boxing certified coach and instructor, and author of *Boxing for Everyone*.

How to Jump from a Building into a Dumpster
Source: Christopher Caso.

How to Avoid and Survive a Hit and Run
Source: Christopher Caso.

How to Break Down a Door
Source: David M. Lowell is a certified master locksmith and education/proficiency registration program manager of the Associated Locksmiths of America, an industry trade group.

How to Survive a Mugging
Source: George Arrington, self-defense instructor, has taught classes in self-defense for more than 25 years and holds a 4th-degree Black Belt and formal teaching license in Danzan-Ryu Jujutsu.

How to Survive if Your Parachute Fails to Open
Source: Joe Jennings is a skydiving cinematographer and skydiving coordination specialist who has designed, coordinated, and filmed skydiving stunts for numerous television commercials, including Mountain Dew, Pepsi, MTV Sports, Coca-Cola, and ESPN.

How to Jump from a Moving Train
Source: Christopher Caso.

How to Survive if You Are Attacked by Leeches
Source: Mark E. Siddall is Assistant Curator for the Division of Invertebrate Zoology at the American Museum of Natural History in New York City.

How to Find Your Direction without a Compass
Sources: Jeff Randall and Mike Perrin, survival experts, run Randall's Adventure and Training (www.jungletraining.com), a service that guides extreme expeditions and facilitates training in the jungles of Central America and the Amazon basin of Peru; *U.S. Army Survival Manual*.

How to Perform a Fast 180-Degree Turn with Your Car
Sources: Vinny Minchillo, demolition derby driver and contributor to a variety of automobile magazines including *AutoWeek*, *SportsCar*, and *Turbo*; Thomas W. Simons, former U.S. Ambassador to Pakistan, and his wife Margaret.

How to Survive a Flash Flood
Source: Federal Emergency Management Administration Office of Meteorology; National Weather Service.

How to Survive When You Fall into a Cesspool
Source: Dan Friedman is a member of the American Society of Home Inspectors and a recipient of the ASHI's National President's Award.

How to Escape from Quicksand
Source: Karl S. Kruszelnicki is a Julius Summer Miller Fellow at the School of Physics of the University of Sydney, Australia, and author of several books about physics and natural phenomena, including *Flying Lasers, Robofish, Cities of Slime, and Other Brain-Bending Science Moments.*

How to Fend Off a Shark
Sources: George H. Burgess, director of the International Shark Attack File at the Florida Museum of Natural History at the University of Florida; Craig Ferreira, board member, Cape Town's South African White Shark Research Institute, a nonprofit organization dedicated to research of the white shark and the preservation of its environment.

How to Escape from a Sinking Car
Sources: The U.S. Army's Cold Regions Research and Engineering Lab in New Hampshire; *Danger! Thin Ice*, a publication of the Minnesota Department of Natural Resources; Tim Smalley.

How to Deal with a Charging Bull
Source: Coleman Cooney is director of the California Academy of Tauromaquia in San Diego.

How to Survive a Plane Crash
Source: William D. Waldock, Professor of Aeronautical Science at Embry-Riddle Aeronautical University and Associate Director of the Center for Aerospace Safety Education at ERAU-Prescott, AZ, has completed more than 75 field investigations and over 200 accident analyses and currently manages the Robertson Aviation Safety Center.

How to Pass a Bribe in a Foreign Country
Source: Jack Viorel, a teacher, has lived and worked throughout Central and South America.

How to Survive in a Plummeting Elevator
Sources: Jay Preston, CSP, PE, general safety engineering consultant and forensic safety engineering specialist, and former president of the Los Angeles chapter of the American Society of Safety Engineers, Larry Holt, Senior Consultant at Elcon Elevator Controls and Consulting in Connecticut.

How to Survive When You Fall through Ice
Source: Tim Smalley.

How to Survive a Sandstorm
Sources: Thomas E. Gill, Adjunct Professor in the Department of Geosciences and a Research Associate at the Wind Engineering Research Center of Texas Tech University; Jeffrey A. Lee, Associate Professor in the Department of Economics and Geography at Texas Tech. Gill and Lee are members of the Texas Wind Erosion Research PersonS (TWERPS), an informal research group of scientists and engineers from the U.S. Department of Agriculture and Texas Tech who study blowing sand and dust storms. The Office of Meteorology, National Weather Service; the U.S. Army Medical Research & Material Command.

How to Make a Raft
Sources: Jeff Randall and Mike Perrin.

How to Escape from Killer Bees
Source: The Texas Agricultural Extension Service.

How to Survive Adrift at Sea
Source: Greta Schanen is managing editor of *Sailing* magazine.

How to Ram Your Car through a Barricade
Source: Vinny Minchillo.

How to Deal with a UFO Sighting or Abduction
Source: The Society for the Preservation of Alien Contact Evidence and Geographic Exploration (SPACEAGE), a grassroots organization dedicated to preserving the nation's extraterrestrial points of interest. The society is the author of *UFO USA: A Traveler's Guide to UFO Sightings, Abduction Sites, Crop Circles, and Other Unexplained Phenomena.*

How to Purify Water
Source: Andrew P. Jenkins, Ph.D., is a member of Central Washington Mountain Rescue and the Yakima County Wilderness Medical Strike Team, and is certified as a Wilderness Emergency Medical Technician.

How to Control a Runaway Camel
Source: Philip Gee, safari operator, runs Explore the Outback, a safari group that leads nature tours of Australia on camelback (www.austcamel.com.au/explore.htm).

How to Jump from Roof to Roof
Source: Christopher Caso.

How to Climb out of a Well
Sources: Andrew P. Jenkins; John Wehbring, mountaineering instructor for the San Diego Mountain Rescue Team, former chairman of the Mountain Rescue Association (California region) and teacher of the Sierra Club's Basic Mountaineering course; Jon Lloyd, adventure consultant with VLM Adventure Consultants in Great Britain (www.vlmadventureconsultants.co.uk).

How to Survive a Trip Over a Waterfall
Sources: Jon Turk; Christopher Macarak.

How to Deal with a Downed Power Line
Source: Larry Holt.

How to Stop a Car with Failed Brakes
Source: Vinny Minchillo.

How to Treat a Scorpion Sting
Source: Scott Stockwell, a major in the United States Army, works as a combat medical entomologist at Fort Sam Houston, TX, consulting on scorpion envenomation. He holds a Ph.D. in Entomology from the University of California, Berkeley.

How to Safely Ram a Car Out of Your Way
Sources: Sam Toler, auto mechanic, demolition derby driver, and member of the Internet Demolition Derby Association; *Car Talk*, a weekly radio program about car repair broadcast on National Public Radio; Thomas W. and Margaret Simons.

How to Escape from an Alligator
Sources: Lynn Krikland, curator of the St. Augustine Alligator Farm; Tim Williams, alligator wrestler and trainer at Orlando's Gatorland.

How to Cross a Piranha-Infested River
Sources: Paul Cripps, Director of Amazonas Explorer; Dr. David Schleser, researcher and eco-travel guide, author of *Piranhas: Everything About Selection, Care, Nutrition, Diseases, Breeding, and Behavior (More Complete Pet Owner's Manuals)*; Barry Tedder, marine biologist and jungle survival expert; Dr. Peter Henderson, director of Pisces Conservation Ltd., Lymington, England.

How to Disable a Car
Source: Lawrence Price is an auto mechanic and conversion van specialist. He received the Under Construction Class Award at the East Coast Nationals Custom Car Show in 1998 and 1999.

How to Identify and Avoid Minefields
Source: Real World Rescue is a small, high-risk travel security consultancy that trains elite U.S. Government Specialist Operations personnel and Federal law enforcement agents.

How to Lose Someone Who Is Following You
Sources: Robert Cabral, self-defense instructor and founder of The International Academy of Martial Arts in West Los Angeles; Brad Binder, Ph.D., Vice President of W. R. Associates, a security firm based in Wisconsin.

About the Authors

Joshua Piven, a computer journalist and freelance writer, has been chased by knife-wielding motorcycle bandits, stuck in subway tunnels, robbed and mugged, has had to break down doors and pick locks, and his computer crashes regularly. He is the co-author of *The Worst-Case Scenario Survival Handbook* (Chronicle, 1999) and *The Worst-Case Scenario Survival Handbook: Travel* (Chronicle, 2001) and lives in Philadelphia with his wife.

David Borgenicht is the president of book soup publishing, a book creation company, and the author of several books, including *The Worst-Case Scenario Survival Handbook* (Chronicle, 1999) and *The Worst-Case Scenario Survival Handbook: Travel* (Chronicle, 2001), both with Joshua Piven; *The Jewish Mother Goose* (Running Press, 2000); and *The Little Book of Stupid Questions* (Hysteria, 1999). He has ridden in heavily armored vehicles in Pakistan, stowed away on Amtrak, and broken into several houses (each for good reason). He, too, lives in Philadelphia with his wife.

Brenda Brown is a freelance illustrator and cartoonist whose work has appeared in many books and major publications, including *The Worst-Case Scenario Survival Handbook* (Chronicle, 1999), *Reader's Digest*, *The Saturday Evening Post*, *The National Enquirer*, and *Federal Lawyer and National Review*. Her digital graphics have been incorporated into software programs developed by Adobe Systems, Deneba Software, Corel Corp., and many Web sites.

Check out www.worstcasescenarios.com for new scenarios, updates, and more! (Because you just never know. . . .)